GDPR Made Si

A practical guide to
implementation of GDPR

Keith Budden IAPP IAAP

In this book, Keith provides an easy-to-follow course in the basics of GDPR, freshly updated for UK GDPR following its introduction at the beginning of 2021.

This book will guide you through all the fundamentals of GDPR, including data capture, data storage, how to conduct a GDPR Data Privacy Impact Assessment, how to respond to a GDPR Data Subject Access Request and what to do if you are unfortunate enough to suffer a data breach.

Written in non-technical language, this book will take you from no knowledge of GDPR to being 100% UK GDPR compliant within your organisation.

The book includes links to useful templates for you to download to implement GDPR successfully within your organisation, and of course it also tells you how to contact the author directly if you need professional help during the implementation within your organisation.

Keep up to date with the latest GDPR news via our monthly newsletter – sign up at
https://gdprmadesimple.club/newsletter

Copyright © 2021 Keith Budden IAPP IAAP

All rights reserved.

No part of this publication may be reproduced, distributed, or transmitted in any form or by any means, including photocopying, recording, or other electronic or mechanical methods, without the prior written permission of the author, except in the case of brief quotations embodied in critical reviews and certain other non-commercial uses permitted by copyright law.

First edition: October 2021

ISBN: 9798757705323

Imprint: Independently published

Disclaimer

This book contains general information based on GDPR and UK GDPR and although I have used every endeavour to ensure that the content is accurate and up to date, readers should seek appropriate legal advice before taking or refraining from taking any action based on the content of this book or otherwise.

The contents of this book do not constitute legal advice and are provided for general information purposes only. If you require specific legal advice you should contact a specialist lawyer. I can only advise on the basis of specific client instructions and am unable to offer legal advice by email to people who are not our clients. To find out more about becoming a client of Ensurety please contact us using the contact details towards the rear of this book.

Ensurety and Keith Budden as an individual accept no responsibility for any information contained within this book and disclaims and excludes any liability in respect of the contents or for action taken based on this information.

Contents

Why GDPR?..1
Principles of GDPR..5
Does it affect my business? 13
Key questions you need to ask 15
Mapping your data and processes 19
Some notes about Privacy Policies 23
Tell me about a DPO...25
Am I a Data Controller or a Data Processor?...............29
Transferring data to your Data Processors.................35
Creating a Data Retention Policy..................................41
Completing a Data Privacy Impact Assessment (DPIA) . 45
"I do" – the wonders of consent 51
Do I always need consent to process data? 57
Dealing with Data Subject Access Requests...............61
So, what happens after you've satisfied a Data Subject Access Request?...69
The Right to be Forgotten..71
AI AI? 73
The Right to Stop Processing 75
Just what is a Data Breach?...77
Dealing with a Data Breach...81
Do I need an EU or UK GDPR agent? 97
Fees and Penalties 101
So, what of the future? 103
Useful resources 109
Sample Privacy Policy 111

Glossary 125
About the author 129

Why GDPR?

Ask many business people in the UK when **GDPR** started and 95% of them will say 25th May 2018, 4% will say 25th May 2016 and 1% will say 23rd March 2012.

In fact they would all be wrong; **GDPR** can be traced right back to a EC directive 95/46/EC which was adopted on 24th October 1995! It's true though that things didn't really build a head of steam until a working party was assembled in 2012 with the rather inglorious title of Working Party 29, which was given the unenviable task of harmonising the data protection rules across the whole of the European Union. Their estimate back in 2012 was that it would take around 3 years to do, so they weren't far off (in **EU** terms) by having it all ready for 25th May 2016. The **EU** then gave all member states 2 years to adopt the regulations into their National laws so that the whole thing could go live on 25th May 2018. That date was achieved although technically not all **EU** countries had got the whole of **GDPR** into their National laws by then.

Of course, way back in 1995, and even from 2012 to 2016, Brexit was something of a pipedream, supported by people like Nigel Farage but hardly something most people in the **UK** (and definitely people in the **EU**) thought would never come to a referendum, let alone actually be achieved.

Fast forward to 2021 and of course Brexit has happened, the **UK** has left the European Union and so from 11 pm on 31st December 2020, the rules in the **UK** became **UK GDPR**. It took the European Union a few more months to declare **UK GDPR** 'adequate' for **EU** countries and the **UK** to share data without restrictions but that brings us to where we are today.

Now, as you will see towards the end of this book, the **UK** Government has launched a public consultation on the future of data protection in the **UK**, and a proposed map for the future of **UK GDPR**.

My personal view is that a lot of the proposed changes are playing with words and that the underlying theme will not change too much. I certainly hope that is the case, since if we (the **UK**) change **GDPR** too much, the **EU** will invoke a clause in their adequacy statement which will potentially mean that overnight, **UK GDPR** will be declared inadequate, and suddenly every single contract involving data transfer between the **EU** and the **UK** will need rewriting to include **Standard Contractual Clauses** and **Binding Corporate Rules**. Not sure what those are? check out the **Glossary** towards the back of this book. Suffice to say they would cause major disruption to data flows, a significant hit to some sectors of the **UK** economy and a great deal of work for **GDPR** practitioners like myself.

Ultimately the only people to really gain from that situation would be **GDPR** practitioners (hooray!) and lawyers (boo!) but seriously, we would all lose, so let's hope it doesn't happen.

So, taking where we are right now, has **GDPR** achieved its aims? Overall, I would say YES it has. It's not perfect, a few parts of it suffer from the law of unintended consequences, but taken as a whole, it works.

It is viewed by some as being the toughest Data Protection regime in the world. I'm not sure that's true, it's robust, yes, but there is nothing within it which is out of reach of any business or organisation which is prepared to invest a few hours to get it right. And you must be one of those people, right? Because otherwise you wouldn't have read this far.

What is certain, is that **GDPR** has in many ways established itself as the platinum standard of Data Protection regimes. It is deeply encouraging to see the number of other data protection regimes emerging around the world which are wholly or largely based on the same principles of **GDPR**.

Whether it is the California Consumer Protection Act, the new data protection laws in Japan, the recently adopted data protection laws in China, or the emerging data protection laws in India, they all have strong connections to **GDPR**.

Is the aim of a universal data protection standard globally still a pipedream? Possibly, but with every new announcement of data protection laws worldwide, we are I think achieving a situation where we will be 80-90% of the way there. Yes, there may be some small regional variations, but the central message remains the same, that it is the protection of data belonging to each individual citizen that is put at the forefront of global data protection regimes.

But enough of what it is, how we got here and where we are now, what you want to know is how you can best implement **UK GDPR** in your organisation, as efficiently and simply as possible.

I'm a **GDPR** practitioner, but I know for most busy business people you don't want to know every single schedule of **GDPR** verbatim, you want a no nonsense, straight talking, how-to book. Ladies and Gentlemen, I present to you **GDPR Made Simple**, start turning these pages and making it happen.

I would love to hear your feedback by the way, so please don't hesitate to email me at
feedback@gdprmadesimple.club

Once again, thanks for buying this book, I hope you enjoy the ride....

Principles of GDPR

There are 6 key principles shared by both **UK GDPR** and **EU GDPR**. Let's look at each of those principles and what they mean in practice.

All personal data must be processed lawfully, fairly and in a transparent manner in relation to the data subject;

The 'data subject' is the person the data is about. For the purposes of **UK GDPR** and **GDPR** this is anyone who is a living person, who lives or works within the **UK** or the **EEA**.

There are extra rules around the data relating to children (and from 2nd September 2021, a child within the scope of **UK GDPR** is anyone under 18 years of age).

For any person who falls under the scope of **GDPR** and/or **UK GDPR**, this first principle of **GDPR** means that any organization storing or processing data about you must have a lawful basis for doing so (we will cover the lawful bases later in this book), they must deal with that data fairly, and anything they do with your data should be explained to you in simple terms that are easy to understand.

All personal data must be collected for specified, explicit, and legitimate purposes and not further processed in a manner that is incompatible with those processes.

The aim of this principle of **GDPR** and **UK GDPR** is to prevent 'fishing expeditions'. What it means in practice is that any organization collecting or storing data about you can only do so if it can prove it has an immediate (or very imminent) need to store that information.

What does that mean in reality? Let's suppose we are building a client database and we think we might, at some point in the future hold a client golf day (although we at the moment have no idea when that might be or even if it will happen, it's just a pipedream), unless and until that becomes a firm reality, we have absolutely zero justification in asking our clients whether or not they enjoy playing golf, and therefore we cannot and should not ask the question.

If, two years down the line, we decide that we really do want to hold a client golf day, then at that point we can ask our clients whether they enjoy playing golf and would like to take part in our golf day. Even then, once the golf day has happened, unless we are planning another golf day, or unless our business is providing golf lessons, a golf course, or golf equipment, we have no justifiable reason for retaining in our database details of who amongst our clients / prospects enjoys playing golf.

All personal data must be adequate, relevant, and limited to what is necessary in relation to the purposes for which it is processed.

In many ways, this principle is identical to the previous principle. Again, it means that we should think about every single field of data we hold about someone and be clear in our own mind that we have a justifiable reason for holding that field of data.

A common exercise I often ask my clients to do is gather your team together (or if you're a sole trader then find a quiet place to sit and think) and look at each field of data you hold about people and give your reason for storing it.

If between you, you can't come up with a valid reason for storing it within 24 seconds, put it on a list.

When you've been through every field of information, take a look at your list. Now, for each item on the list, consider for up to 24 minutes whether you can come up with a valid reason for storing that data item. If, after 24 minutes you can't come up with a valid reason for keeping it, put it on a second list.

Once you've been through every field on your list and either noted a valid reason for keeping that field or you have put the field on your second list, put the second list to one side for 24 hours.

When you return to the second list 24 hours later, again give yourselves 24 minutes to think why you keep that field of information. If within those 24 minutes you still (either individually if you're doing this on your own, or as a team), cannot think of a valid reason why you are holding that field of data, you probably should not be holding it and should erase that field of data from your database / customer relationship management (**CRM**) system.

All personal data must be accurate and where necessary kept up to date; every reasonable step must be taken to ensure that personal data that is inaccurate, is erased or rectified without delay.

This is essential. As a rule, the more recent data is, the more accurate that data is.

So, what does this principle mean in practice?

Firstly, it is worthwhile to set up a regular data review process, which typically will be done annually.

You should use this process to determine what data may need updating and by referring to your **Data Retention Policy** (we will come to that later in this book) determine what data needs to be deleted.

Secondly, if someone contacts you, either voluntarily or in response to either a query from you and/or that you have satisfied a **Data Subject Access Request (DSAR)** for that person (we will cover Data Subject Access Requests later in this book too), you have 30 days to correct that information.

Whether you choose to update data as individual items, or you batch changes together is up to you, as long as if the change has been notified to you by the **Data Subject**, then you action that change within 30 days of receipt.

All personal data must be kept in a form which permits identification of data subjects for no longer than is necessary for the purposes for which the personal data is processed.

In many ways, this ties in with your **Data Retention Policy**.

Let's take a practical example.

Assume you sell bicycles, and your bicycles have a 3-year warranty. You keep a record of each sale which includes the customer's name, address, the bike model, and the chassis number of the bicycle (so that if the customer makes a claim under the warranty, you can be sure that the bicycle came from you).

After those 3 years have elapsed, you no longer have a justifiable reason (under **GDPR** and/or **UK GDPR**) to retain the chassis number (or indeed the customer's name and address assuming they've bought nothing else from you in the interim time period), and so you should anonymise their record so that anyone looking at the record cannot identify who is the person concerned. By anonymizing the record, you can retain the bike model, which could of course be useful to you at some future point for analysing how many of each bike model you have sold.

Be careful when anonymising records. Again, using the above example let's suppose a typical record in our client warranty file is as below:

Customer code: ABC123

Customer name: Mr John Doe

Customer address: 23 Acacia Avenue, Anytown, AA1 1AA

Date of purchase: 10/10/2021

Model: Chopper

Serial No: AJ39202100

When we come to anonymise this record, the immediate thought is, well if we make the record as below, we've anonymised it: -

Customer code: ABC123

Date of purchase: 10/10/2021

Model: Chopper

That's a step in the right direction, but it's not anonymized enough yet. Why? Because if I have that record, and I also have your invoices which identify customer ABC123 and give me their name and address, then the record is no longer anonymous.

So, what we need to end up with is a record as below:

Customer code: XXXXXX

Date of purchase: 10/10/2021

Model: Chopper

Hopefully that now makes sense and indicates why anonymising data is not as simple as it first appears.

All personal data must be processed in a manner that ensures appropriate security of the personal data, including protection against unauthorized or unlawful processing and against accidental loss, destruction, or damage, using appropriate organisational and technical measures.

A crucial point to consider here is that **GDPR / UK GDPR** applies to "**all data which is held within a structured filing system**".

So, what does that actually mean?

It means that whether the data is held on a computer system, is held in the cloud, or is handwritten on a sheet of paper, doesn't matter, if it's held within a **structured filing system** then it falls under **GDPR / UK GDPR**.

So, what exactly is a '**structured filing system**'?

My favourite example to illustrate this is for you to imagine that you have just visited a trade exhibition relevant to your industry, you've had a really productive day wandering around, chatting to the various exhibitors, and exchanging business cards with them.

Now, imagine you're back in your office. Do you a) leave the business cards scattered on your desk; b) chuck the business cards into one of the drawers in your desk; or c) put the business cards into a rolodex or into a card filing system.

If your answer is a) or b) then **GDPR / UK GDPR** does not apply to those business cards and the information on them but if your answer is c) then **GDPR / UK GDPR** does apply to those business cards and the information on them as they are now considered to be within a **structured filing system.**

So now we have established what data **GDPR / UK GDPR** refers to, what does **GDPR / UK GDPR** mean when it says, "**appropriate security**".

Again, let's split this into records held electronically on a computer and records held manually on paper.

For records held electronically on a computer, it should always be necessary to enter a password to access the computer. Each employee should have their own username and password and employees should be discouraged from sharing passwords.

For many systems now, it is also considered best practice to implement **multi-factor authentication** (**MFA**) (also referred to as **two factor authentication (2FA)**).

So, what about records held manually on paper?

These records should be securely locked away whenever they are not in use (i.e., overnight, or whenever you are away from your desk for a period of time).

By the way – being securely locked away does not mean that you put them in a filing cabinet or cupboard which has a lock on it, but they key to that cabinet has been lost in the midst of time. If you don't have the key (or combination if it's a combination lock), then you haven't locked them away. Technically, that's a breach of **GDPR / UK GDPR**, so invest in a new lock and make sure you use the key.

With the growing use of homeworking since the Covid-19 pandemic, it is accepted that many employees may not have somewhere that records can be locked away overnight.

In the short term, while we were mid pandemic, it was accepted that it was reasonable for these employees to place the records out of sight in either a drawer or cupboard when they were not in use. However, now that the situation is settling down, that is no longer adequate. If your employee does not have a lockable cabinet to store paper records in, it's time for your organisation to invest in one for them. While you're at it, get them a decent cross-cut shredder as well (see the **Useful Resources** section of this book for ideas on suitable shredders). We will return to the issue of shredders later when we discuss **Data Retention Policies**.

Does it affect my business?

This is probably the simplest question in the whole book.

If you have clients or employees within the **UK** or **European Economic Area** (**EEA**) or other individuals within the **UK** or **European Economic Area** (**EEA**) on whom you hold data, then **UK GDPR** and/or **EU GDPR** applies to your business.

It really is that simple, no if's, no but's.

The common question that comes after that is "but we are not based in the **UK** or **EEA** so does **GDPR** and/or **UK GDPR** still apply to us?" The answer to that is yes it does, whether your business or organization is based in Toulouse, Tennessee, or Timbuktu, really doesn't matter, if you are storing or processing data about people who live and/or work within the **UK** and/or **EEA**, then **GDPR** applies to you.

Of course, if you are based outside of the **UK**, there may be other local data protection laws that apply to you too, but they are outside the scope of this book.

Key questions you need to ask

I call these key questions the 5 'W's and it will soon become apparent why.

Who do I hold data on?

If you have employees, then the first answer to this is obvious, it is your employees.

Equally, you probably have clients, and you will be holding data on them too.

But chances are you hold data on lots of other individuals too, depending on how your organisation is set up, you may well hold details of suppliers, shareholders, fundraisers, and volunteers.

The list goes on, grab a sheet of paper now and spend a few minutes just making a list of who you hold data on.

What information do you hold about them?

We will cover this more in the **Mapping your data and processes** chapter, but for now just think in general terms what information you hold about the people you identified in the list above. Again, on your sheet of paper, just note down in outline form the data you hold about each person (and remember of course that information may be different depending upon the role of that person).

Why do I hold that information / What do I do with it?

Again, we will cover this more in the **Mapping your data and processes** chapter but think in general terms at the moment. Against each item you identified in the list above, make a note of why you hold that information and what you do with it. You might find it useful to use different colour pens or post-it notes for this part of the process.

Where is it stored?

At a top level, for each of the data types you identified, is it held electronically on a computer or other device, or is it held on to paper.

Once you've got that far, then get more precise about where it is stored, for example, for computer data, is it encrypted? Is it regularly backed up? Do you know how to restore a backup? Have you tested it?

For paper documents, where do you keep them? Does the lock on their filing cabinet/cupboard actually work? Have you got duplicates somewhere in case a fire or other disaster affected your workplace?

When do I destroy it?

As you will discover in the **Creating a Data Retention Policy** chapter of this book, a key principle of **GDPR / UK GDPR** is that each data field has a data life.

For now, just think in general terms about the data you have identified. When do you destroy it? How do you destroy it? How do you record that you have destroyed it?

So, to recap – here are the 5 W's again (ok technically it's 6 but two of them just sit naturally together)

Who do I hold data on?

What information do I hold about them?

Why do I hold that information / What do I do with it?

Where is it stored?

When do I destroy it?

Mapping your data and processes

Article 30 of **GDPR / UK GDPR** requires you to map your data and data processes so that you can identify where there may be risks to the security of **Personally Identifiable Information**.

When conducting this mapping it is best to start at a really high level and then gradually drill down into the information.

So to begin with, just make a list of all of the organisations your organisation transfers data with – remember that those data transfers might be electronic, they might be on paper, or they may simply be oral.

Once you've made that list (and you may well want to discuss the list with other people within your organisation to ensure you haven't missed anyone off), go through the list and identify those organisations who either send you **Personally Identifiable Information**, or you send them **Personally Identifiable Information**.

Now you have that list, for each of those organisations, walkthrough the information lifecycle for the **Personally Identifiable Information** to/from those organisations. Document this as you go and try to identify any steps where the **Personally Identifiable Information** is vulnerable, either because it is in transit between you and the other organisation, or it's possible that a 'bad actor' could infiltrate a system at that point and gain access to the **Personally Identifiable Information**.

It is a good idea to consult with the organisation you are sending the **Personally Identifiable Information** to or receiving the **Personally Identifiable Information** from to see if they identify any weak spots that you may have missed.

Once you have done that step, then work through the list below for each element of data within the **Personally Identifiable Information**

Data Items

What kind of **Personally Identifiable Information** is being processed (clients, employees etc.)?

Does any of the **Personally Identifiable Information** fall under '**Special Categories**' within **GDPR / UK GDPR**? (see page 26 of this book for details of what is considered '**Special Category**' data)

Data Formats

In what format is the **Personally Identifiable Information** stored (hard copy, digital, database, bring your own device, mobile phones, etc.)

Transfer Method

How do you collect the **Personally Identifiable Information** and how do you share it, both internally within your organisation and externally with other organisations.

Storage Location

What locations are involved within the data flow (offices, the Cloud, third parties, etc.)?

Accountability

Who is accountable for the personal data? Often this changes as the data moves throughout your organisation or to and from other external organisations.

Access

Who has access to this **Personally Identifiable Information**?

Lawful Basis

Identify which lawful basis you are relying on to allow you to process this **Personally Identifiable Information**? You can find more details about lawful basis and **GDPR / UK GDPR** in the **Do I always need consent to process personal data** chapter in this book.

Document each of your answers as you go.

Well done! You have now completed the mapping of your **Personally Identifiable Information** as required by Article 30 of **GDPR / UK GDPR**. Hopefully it wasn't too time consuming and you now know where and how **Personally Identifiable Information** travels in and out of (and indeed within) your organisation.

Some notes about Privacy Policies

If you have a website, the chances are that your website already has a **Privacy Policy** (don't worry if yours didn't until you read this, a sample **Privacy Policy** is included towards the back of this book and you can also download a template from our **Templates Library** via the **URL** in the **Useful Resources** section of this book).

Even if you do have a **Privacy Policy** on your website, there's every chance it is out of date. If you have been in business since before 25th May 2018, then in the majority of cases you will probably have had a **GDPR** compliant **Privacy Policy** put on your website then and have never updated it since.

A generalisation I know, but it is far more common than you might think. You really should have had your **Privacy Policy** reviewed since 31st December 2020 to ensure it remains in compliance with **UK GDPR**. Again, please feel free to use the policy accessible via our **Templates Library**.

I'm not going to go through the wording of the **Privacy Policy** paragraph by paragraph, you can easily read the sample **Privacy Policy** towards the back of this book, but I am going to provide you with 3 very useful tips.

Firstly, if you have employees, then you need a separate **Privacy Policy** for your employees than the one on your website. There are conditions which need to be included in an employee **Privacy Policy** which are not in your normal public **Privacy Policy**. Again, please see our **Useful Resources** for details.

Secondly, while you may well have your **Privacy Policy** on your website, it is worthwhile to have some printed copies of your **Privacy Policy** too. Print them and if possible laminate them so you can have them to hand whenever you might need them. An example would be if you have a stand at a trade exhibition, or you are a retail shop, having a physical copy of your **Privacy Policy** you can show to any contact who requests it is not only a good idea, it's great customer service too.

Thirdly, and most importantly, always ensure your **Privacy Policy** includes the **Effective Date**, i.e. the date from which this **Privacy Policy** applies. Why? Because the **Privacy Policy** which applies to any data you hold or process is the **Privacy Policy** which was in force when you collected that data.

So, to give an example, let's suppose you have a **Privacy Policy** which came into effect on 25th May 2018, and then you revise the **Privacy Policy** to bring it into line with **UK GDPR** on 2nd February 2021. Any data collected between 25th May and 1st February 2021 falls under your old **Privacy Policy**, only data collected on or after the 2nd February 2021 falls under the new one. This can be crucial if you have a **Data Subject** who complains that you have not complied with your **Privacy Policy** at some point in the future.

Tell me about a DPO

It is your **Data Protection Officer** (**DPO**)'s job to ensure that GDPR is correctly established and operates correctly on a day-to-day basis. Often your **DPO** will also perform training on an annual basis for all of your staff, and as necessary for new starters in your organisation (although this may be outsourced to an external provider).

So, could my Managing Director be our DPO?

No, nor could any of your directors who have a financial interest in the organisation (i.e., they have shares in the business and/or they receive a performance bonus as a substantial portion of their income).

GDPR and UK GDPR state that the DPO must be someone who does not have a financial interest in the company. That doesn't mean you don't pay them a salary (or a fee if they are external to your organisation), but they can't have shares in your organisation or have a profit share as a substantial portion of their income).

So why does it matter whether they have shares?

Because the DPO must always act in the best interest of the **Data Subjects**.

Let's look at an example. Your organisation, XYZ Data Services, has come up with a new algorithm which will rapidly assess someone's eligibility for a loan, but it will do this completely automatically, there will be no opportunity to appeal, and the data will be shared automatically with the credit reference agency and the finance company providing the loan, all without any consent being gained from the applicant. This new algorithm and process is going to make a profit for XYZ Data Services of at least £1 million per year.

The **DPO** should instantly tell XYZ Data Services that they can't do that proposed process as it breaches GDPR in several different areas. However, the **DPO** has 20% of the shares in XYZ Data Services and so they stand to potentially make £200,000 per year from this new process. They decide to 'turn a blind eye' to the process and let XYZ Data Services proceed with their plans.

However, if the **DPO** has no financial interest in whether the new process is implemented or not, they conduct a **Data Privacy Impact Assessment (DPIA)** and as an outcome of the **DPIA**, they will tell XYZ Data Services that they cannot implement their planned process as it breaches GDPR.

Don't worry at the moment if you don't know what a **DPIA** is, I will cover those in much greater depth later in this book.

Do I have to have a DPO?

Under UK GDPR, you must appoint a DPO if: -

- you are a public authority or body (except for courts acting in their judicial capacity).

- your core activities require large scale, regular and systematic monitoring of individuals (for example, online behaviour tracking); or

- your core activities consist of large-scale processing of special categories of data or data relating to criminal convictions and offences.

Special categories of data relate to things like, medical data, payroll data, whether someone is a member of a political party, whether someone is a member of a trade union and since 2nd September 2021, all data relating to anyone under 18 years of age.

So, what does large scale mean? There is no absolute definition as it varies from situation to situation.

To give an example:

Company A has one retail shop selling bicycles. They are situated in a quiet village and sell no more than 3 bicycles per day. They have a mailing list of approximately 300 customers and former customers.

Company B also sells bicycles, but they are in a busy out of town retail park, they have 10 similar branches across the UK and each shop sells at least 100 bicycles per day, some of which are sales via their buy now, pay later scheme. They have a mailing list of 200,000 people and also operate a bicycle loyalty scheme which has 50,000 people signed up.

Company A would not be regarded as large-scale processing and so would not legally have to appoint a **Data Protection Officer (DPO)**.

Company B would be regarded as large-scale processing and so would legally have to appoint a **Data Protection Officer (DPO)**.

So, should I appoint a DPO even if the law says I don't have to?

That really is a choice only you can make. I am the external **DPO** for a number of organisations who would not meet the criteria of large-scale processing, but who nonetheless like the peace of mind of having a **DPO** at hand.

Should I have an internal or external DPO?

Of course, I'm going to be biased here and say you should have an external DPO! But, give me a moment to explain why I believe an external DPO is the best choice.

As we stated a couple of pages ago, the **DPO** should always act in the best interest of the **Data Subject**, typically by performing a **Data Privacy Impact Assessment (DPIA)** and communicating the result of that assessment to the management of the organisation.

If your **DPO** is internal to the organisation, even though they satisfy the requirement of not having a financial stake in the business, they will quite naturally, always have one eye on their career progression (whether within the business or elsewhere) and will want to 'keep on the right side' of the senior managers within the organisation. As a result, they may 'tone down' their response within the **DPIA**.

If your **DPO** is external to the organisation, they are more likely to feel empowered to be able to say "STOP" you cannot implement this process or continue running this process, if that is the outcome of the **DPIA**. This is a crucial part of the **DPO**'s role.

I don't agree with my DPO's decision, can I dismiss them and/or terminate their contract?

No. DPOs are protected by law in this situation.

Whether a DPO is internal or external to your organisation, you cannot terminate their contract simply because you don't agree with their judgement on GDPR / UK GDPR matters. You can of course cancel their contract, just like any other, for failure to comply with timescales, or gross misconduct, but not because you don't agree with their GDPR / UK GDPR related decisions.

Am I a Data Controller or a Data Processor?

One of the first things you need to decide, is your organisation a **Data Controller**, a **Data Processor** or both?

Remember that you can be more than one of these at the same time, and indeed, you can even become a **Joint Data Controller** (but we will come on to that later).

So how you do decide if you are a **Data Controller**, a **Data Processor** or a **Joint Data Controller**?

Use the following checklists to help you decide (you can also download copies of these checklists via the link in the **Useful Resources** section of this book.

Don't worry if you can't tick every box under each heading. The important thing is once you have completed the checklist, the category in which you have the highest proportion of boxes ticked is probably the category which you satisfy for that data type.

You need to complete the checklist for each data type that you identified when you mapped out your data and processes. Why? Because you may be a **Data Controller** in one process and a **Data Processor** in another.

To give an example of this, let's assume you are a **Data Processor** for a third-party, but at the same time you have your own employees, so while in terms of the third-party data you are a **Data Processor**, in terms of your employees, you are their **Data Controller.**

Data Controller Checklist

☐ We decided to collect or process the personal data.

☐ We decided what the purpose or outcome of the processing was to be.

☐ We decided what personal data should be collected.

☐ We decided which individuals to collect personal data about.

☐ We obtain a commercial gain or other benefit from the processing, except for any payment for services from another controller.

☐ We are processing the personal data as a result of a contract between us and the data subject.

☐ The data subjects are our employees.

☐ We make decisions about the individuals concerned as part of or as a result of the processing.

☐ We exercise professional judgement in the processing of the personal data.

☐ We have a direct relationship with the data subjects.

☐ We have complete autonomy as to how the personal data is processed.

☐ We have appointed the processors to process the personal data on our behalf.

Data Processor Checklist

☐ We are following instructions from someone else regarding the processing of personal data.

☐ We were given the personal data by a customer or similar third party, or told what data to collect.

☐ We do not decide to collect personal data from individuals.

☐ We do not decide what personal data should be collected from individuals.

☐ We do not decide the lawful basis for the use of that data.

☐ We do not decide what purpose or purposes the data will be used for.

☐ We do not decide whether to disclose the data, or to whom.

☐ We do not decide how long to retain the data.

☐ We may make some decisions on how data is processed, but implement these decisions under a contract with someone else.

☐ We are not interested in the end result of the processing.

Joint Data Controller checklist

☐ We have a common objective with others regarding the processing.

☐ We are processing the personal data for the same purpose as another controller.

☐ We are using the same set of personal data (eg one database) for this processing as another controller.

☐ We have designed this process with another controller.

☐ We have common information management rules with another controller.

To take a practical example, let us suppose that you are an online retailer. Via your website you collect all of the data relating to an order, however you don't maintain any stock yourself, the stock fulfilment is supplied by another company. In this instance you are the **Data Controller** and the fulfilment company is the **Data Processor**.

However, if we now look at the fulfilment company for a moment, while they are a **Data Processor** for the fulfilment of your customer orders, they employ their own staff. For those employee records they are the **Data Controller**.

So, how can two organisations be **Joint Data Controllers**? Again, let's return to our example of the fulfilment company. We have established that they are **Data Processors** for us and **Data Controller** for their employees.

But let's add to that scenario and now assume that the fulfilment company uses a payroll bureau to process the payroll for their employees.

Now, the fulfilment company is the **Data Controller** for the employee data, but the payroll bureau is also a **Data Controller** for the data as they can update the details held on each employee, can update the employee payroll records, produce payslips, send those payslips to the employees etc. So, in this instance, the fulfilment company and the payroll bureau are **Joint Data Controllers**.

Where does liability lie?

In the event of a breach of GDPR and/or UK GDPR, liability for the breach depends on the nature of the breach and where it occurred. But liability can pass from **Data Controller** to **Data Processor** or vice versa.

An example would be where a **Data Processor** suffers a major **Data Breach**. Clearly the **Data Processor** would be liable for any penalties imposed by the **ICO** and any claims for damages from those people affected by the **Data Breach**, but depending on the nature of the information which was lost, the **Data Controller** could also be liable.

To use the example we used before of the fulfilment company and the payroll bureau. If the payroll bureau suffered a major **Data Breach**, the payroll bureau could face **ICO** penalties and claims for damages from your employees involved, but you could also face penalties if that breach now means that you can't fulfil your obligations in terms of reporting to HM Revenue & Customs or being able to answer an employee query regarding their payroll.

The importance of a clear Data Processing Agreement

It is precisely because of scenarios like the one above that it is crucial you have a clear **Data Processing Agreement** between yourselves and any **Data Processors** or **Joint Data Controllers** that you work with. Please see our **Useful Resources** section for more details on **Data Processing Agreements**.

What should I check before appointing a Data Processor?

Recent precedent has established that it is for the **Data Controller** to satisfy themselves that their **Data Processors** are **UK GDPR / GDPR** compliant (or equivalent if the **Data Processor** is based outside of the **UK/EU**).

To do this fully, you should consider commissioning a full **GDPR Audit** of the **Data Processor** (unless they can show you that a recent one has been completed already), and you should also ask each of your **Data Processors** to provide you with an up-to-date copy of their **ICO** registration certificate (or equivalent). Failure to do this is actually a breach of **GDPR / UK GDPR** and could mean you suffer a penalty.

Transferring data to your Data Processors

So, by now you should have established what data you hold and what you do with it.

Now, we have to consider for those areas of **Personally Identifiable Information** which you transfer to your **Data Processors**, where those **Data Processors** are located geographically, how you are going to satisfy yourself that those **Data Processors** are themselves **GDPR / UK GDPR** or equivalent compliant, what contracts / contractual clauses do you need to have in place between you and your **Data Processor**, what actual methods you are going to use for transferring the **Personally Identifiable Information** back and forth, and what responsibilities your **Data Processor** is going to have in the result of either a **Data Subject Access Request** or a **Data Breach**.

Let's look at each of these individually.

Where is the Data Processor located geographically, and just as importantly, where will they store your data geographically?

Assuming you are based in the UK and you are the **Data Controller**, there are a number of scenarios to consider:

a) **the Data Processor is within the UK and is planning to store the Personally Identifiable Information within the UK**

   This is the simplest solution and requires no additional wording in your contract.

b) **the Data Processor is within the UK and is planning to store the Personally Identifiable Information outside of the UK but within the EU**

As the **Personally Identifiable Information** will be stored outside the UK but within the EU, you currently do not need any additional wording in your contract. However, the EU is currently working on the wording of some **Standard Contractual Clauses** for data transfers from/to the UK to/from the EU. It is anticipated that these new **Standard Contractual Clauses** will be approved at some point in 2022, but there will probably be a grace period for their inclusion in any existing contracts until 2023.

c) **the Data Processor is within the UK and is planning to store the Personally Identifiable Information outside of the UK and EU**

As the data is being stored outside of the UK and EU, you must ensure that the relevant **Standard Contractual Clauses** are included within your contract with the **Data Processor**.

d) **the Data Processor is within the EU and is planning to store the Personally Identifiable Information within the UK**

As the **Data Processor** is outside the UK but within the EU, you will need to include the **Standard Contractual Clauses** in your contract. However, please be aware that the EU is currently working on the wording of some new **Standard Contractual Clauses** for data transfers from/to the UK to/from the EU. It is anticipated that these new **Standard Contractual Clauses** will be approved at some point in 2022, but there will probably be a grace period for their inclusion in any existing contracts until 2023.

e) **the Data Processor is within the EU and is planning to store the Personally Identifiable Information outside of the UK but within the EU**

As the **Data Processor** is outside the UK but within the EU, you will need to include the **Standard Contractual Clauses** in your contract. However, please be aware that the EU is currently working on the wording of some new **Standard Contractual Clauses** for data transfers from/to the UK to/from the EU. It is anticipated that these new **Standard Contractual Clauses** will be approved at some point in 2022, but there will probably be a grace period for their inclusion in any existing contracts until 2023.

f) **the Data Processor is within the EU and is planning to store the Personally Identifiable Information outside of the UK and EU**

As the **Data Processor** is outside the UK but within the EU, you will need to include the **Standard Contractual Clauses** in your contract.

g) **the Data Processor is outside of the UK and EU and is planning to store the Personally Identifiable Information within the UK**

As the **Data Processor** is outside of the UK and EU, you will need to include the **Standard Contractual Clauses** in your contract.

h) **the Data Processor is outside of the the UK and is planning to store the Personally Identifiable Information outside of the UK but within the EU**

As the **Data Processor** is outside of the UK and EU, you will need to include the **Standard Contractual Clauses** in your contract.

i) the Data Processor is outside of the UK and is planning to store the Personally Identifiable Information outside of the UK and EU

As the **Data Processor** is outside of the UK and EU, you will need to include the **Standard Contractual Clauses** in your contract.

How are you going to satisfy yourself that the Data Processor is GDPR / UK GDPR compliant (or has a suitable equivalent compliance)?

This can be difficult to achieve 100%, particularly in the current Covid-19 dominated worldwide environment, but it is important that you satisfy yourself that the **Data Processor** is **GDPR / UK GDPR** compliant (or has a suitable equivalent compliance).

At the minimum, if the **Data Processor** is located in and/or the **Personally Identifiable Information** is going to be stored within either the UK or the EU, you should ask to see a copy of their certificate of registration with the **ICO** or the relevant **Data Protection Authority** in the country in which they are based and/or will be storing your data.

If the contract is significant to your organisation, I would strongly suggest that you commission a **GDPR Audit**, either from me (you can find my contact details right at the back of this book) or from another **GDPR Practitioner**.

If you can't justify the investment of a **GDPR Audit**, you should ask the **Data Processor** for a copy of their **GDPR** procedures. Once you receive these copies, check them for compliance (comparing them against the information in this book would be a great start).

Always remember that under **UK GDPR** and now confirmed via court precedent, it is your responsibility as **Data Controller** to satisfy yourself that any **Data Processor** you use are themselves fully **UK GDPR / GDPR / other equivalent** compliant. For this reason, always ensure that you fully document all steps you have taken to satisfy yourself that the **Data Processor** is compliant.

Sometimes, it is necessary to think outside the box. To give you an example, one of my clients makes use of developers in India. They provided all of the documentation requested but we still had a nagging doubt about the physical security of their office in India. In 'normal' times, the client may well have paid for me to get on a plane and travel out to India to look around the premises myself. Of course, Covid-19 made that trip impossible, so how else to do it?

I was watching a programme on TV where someone was wearing a Go-Pro camera on their head. This struck me as the ideal solution, so my client purchased a Go-Pro camera, we shipped it out to India, one of the developers then put the Go-Pro camera on his head, and wandered around their office following our instructions. It was a great way of achieving the desired level of satisfaction (and it was a very cost-effective solution too).

What contracts and/or contractual clauses do you need to have in place with the Data Processor?

As I explained when considering where the **Data Processor** is geographically located, and where the **Data Processor** will store your **Personally Identifiable Information**, you may need to include within any contract either the **UK Standard Contractual Clauses**, the **EU Standard Contractual Clauses**, or a combination of the two.

What actual methods are you going to use to transfer the Personally Identifiable Information back and forth?

If I were to make one, simple request here, it would be please DO NOT transfer **Personally Identifiable Information** to or from your **Data Processor** via email. Email is easily intercepted, or a phishing or other attack may mean that you think you are sending data to your **Data Processor** when in fact you are sending it to an imposter.

Rather than using email, use a Sharepoint drive if you are using Microsoft Office 365, or alternatively use a 3rd party file transfer service such as wetransfer.com.

Even when using Sharepoint or a service like wetransfer.com, I recommend that you compress and encrypt the file(s) you are transferring – an example can be making the files into a .zip file and adding a password to the .zip file. Remember to notify the **Data Processor** of the password via a separate email notification. Do not put the password into the notes field is you use a file transfer service.

What responsibilities will the Data Processor have in the event of a Data Subject Access Request or a Data Breach?

I recommend that you ensure that the **Data Processing Agreement** between yourself and your **Data Processor** is clear on where responsibility will lie should there be a **Data Breach** and also that it sets clear time limits for the **Data Processor** to respond with information to satisfy any **Data Subject Access Requests** that you receive.

Another important point to include in the **Data Processing Agreement** are clear instructions to the **Data Processor** on what they should do if a **Data Subject** submits a **Data Subject Access Request** direct to the **Data Processor** concerning **Personally Identifiable Information** the **Data Processor** is holding on your behalf. I would recommend that you use the **Data Processing Agreement** to tell the **Data Processor** that they must notify you of any such requests within 24 hours of receipt and that the **Data Processor** must not directly respond to the **Data Subject** without your express agreement.

Creating a Data Retention Policy

One of the key principles of **GDPR** and **UK GDPR** is that every data element has a data life.

What does that mean in practice? It means looking at each of the data types you identified when you mapped your data and processes and determining how long you actually need to keep that data *in a personally identifiable form* for.

For some data types, the decision is easy, it's laid down in law, for example, the law says how long accounting records must be retained, and how long payroll records must be retained.

However, for other data types, there are no hard and fast rules, it really is up to you to decide, but do set aside some time specifically to set these time limits, discuss them with colleagues and if necessary seek outside advice from a **GDPR** practitioner like myself. Remember at some point in the future you may be asked by a **Data Subject** or by the **ICO** to justify why you made your decision, so make sure for each data type you document your decision making process.

I will give you a practical example: -

One of my clients is a Championship League football club. They needed to decide how long they were going to retain their personnel records.

For the majority of staff this was an easy decision, they would keep the data for the whole period the person was employed by the club, plus a further six years, to allow for any enquiries by Her Majesty's Revenue and Customs or any action brought at a tribunal by the employee themselves.

However, for players and managers this was a harder decision. For contractual reasons, the club wished to keep records of each player or manager for the length of that player's career. For this reason they decided 70 years would be a reasonable time period to retain player and manager records (on the basis that even if someone had joined the club as a youth player at 14 years of age, an additional 70 years would make the person 84 years old, at which age they would certainly no longer be playing professional football and they were unlikely to still be a paid manager at any football club).

However, the club's official historian and archivist then became involved and it became apparent that it could be necessary to provide player information further back than 70 years if someone was writing a history of the club or a biography of an individual player. As a result of this intervention, the decision was made to extend the data retention period for players and managers to 100 years. This was considered adequate as the chance of a player living for 100 years from their date of signing for the club was considered minimal, and since **GDPR** and **UK GDPR** only apply to living persons, the chance of a player or manager being deceased by the time the 100 year anniversary arose was considered sufficiently high that any further extension could not reasonably be justified.

So to implement a **GDPR Data Retention Policy**, there are three key steps.

1. Decide how long you are going to retain data for each data type.

2. Draw up your **Data Retention Policy**, clearly setting out how long you are going to retain each data type, and document your decision making process for how you came to those conclusions.

3. Ensure you make someone responsible for ensuring that your **Data Retention Policy** is adhered to. This is one reason that I advise against having really short document retention periods.

The reason it is important that you have someone responsible for ensuring that the **Data Retention Policy** is adhered to, is that failing to adhere to your **Data Retention Policy** can, and does, result in your organisation receiving penalties for a breach of **GDPR / UK GDPR**.

If you have an audit from the **ICO**, or you commission a **GDPR** Practitioner like myself to conduct an audit, and your **Document Retention Policy** says you retain let's say Client contact records for 3 years, and the auditor finds a Client contact record which is 5 years old, you will fail your **GDPR** audit.

Completing a Data Privacy Impact Assessment (DPIA)

DPIA – the four-letter acronym that strikes fear into everyone connected with **GDPR**!

I'm joking! **Data Privacy Impact Assessments** (also sometimes called **Data Protection Impact Assessments**) really don't need to be frightening. If you approach them in a logical way, they really are quite straightforward and should only take you an hour or two to complete for each of the processes you identified during the **Mapping your data and processes** chapter of this book (If you've not completed that chapter yet, go back and do it now as the rest of this chapter will make much more sense once you've completed that one).

Remember that as well as completing a **DPIA** for each of your current processes, every time you introduce a new process to your business or modify an existing process which impacts upon (or could impact upon) **Personally Identifiable Information**, complete a fresh **DPIA**.

So, grab yourself a cup of your favourite brew, pen and paper at the ready.

Step 1: Identify the need for a DPIA

Explain broadly what the data process you are considering aims to achieve and what type of processing it involves. You may find it helpful to refer or link to other documents, such as a project proposal. Summarise why you identify the need for a **DPIA**.

Step 2: Describe the nature of the processing:

How will you collect, use, store and delete **Personally Identifiable Information**?

What is the source of the **Personally Identifiable Information**?

Will you be sharing **Personally Identifiable Information** with anyone?

You might find it useful to refer to a flow diagram as another way of describing the data flows.

Would you consider that any of the processing identified involves a high risk to the **Personally Identifiable Information**?

Step 3: Describe the scope of the processing:

What is the nature of the **Personally Identifiable Information**, and does it include special category or criminal offence information?

How much **Personally Identifiable Information** will you be collecting and using?

How often will you be collecting and using **Personally Identifiable Information**?

How long will you retain the **Personally Identifiable Information**?

How many individuals are affected?

What geographical area does it cover?

Step 4: Describe the context of the processing:

What is the nature of your relationship with the individuals?

How much control will the individuals have over their data?

Would the individuals involved expect you to use their data in this way?

Do they include children or other vulnerable groups?

Could your new process be considered to be novel in any way?

Do you have any prior concerns over this type of processing or its potential security flaws?

What is the current state of technology in the area this process covers? Is it old and therefore likely to become redundant, or is it cutting edge and therefore potentially vulnerable?

Are there any current issues of public concern that you should factor in?

Is the new process covered by any approved code of conduct or certification scheme and if so, are you signed up to any such code of conduct?

Step 5: Describe the purposes of the processing

What do you want to achieve?

What is the intended effect (if any) on individuals?

What are the benefits of the processing for you? and more broadly?

Step 6: Consultation

Consider how to consult with relevant stakeholders:
Describe when and how you will seek individuals' views – or justify why it's not appropriate to do so.

Who else do you need to involve within you organisation?

Do you need to ask any external data processors to assist?

Do you plan to consult information security experts, or any other experts?

Step 7: Assess necessity and proportionality

What is your lawful basis for processing?

(You can find more details about each legal basis in the **Do I always need consent to process data** chapter of this book)

Does the processing actually achieve your purpose?

Is there another way to achieve the same outcome?

How will you prevent function creep?

How will you ensure data quality and data minimisation?

What information will give you individuals?

How will you help to support their rights?

What measures do you take to ensure **Data Processors** comply with **GDPR / UK GDPR**?

How do you safeguard any international transfers?

Step 8: Identify and assess risks

For each risk that you have identified:

Describe the source of the risk and the nature of the potential impact on individuals. Include associated compliance and corporate risk as necessary.

Identify the likelihood of harm - is it remote, possible or probable?

Identify the severity of harm – is it minimal, significant or severe?

Identify the overall risk – is it low, medium or high?

Step 9: Identify measures to reduce risk

For each risk you have identified at step 8:

Identify any options there may be to reduce or eliminate the risk

For each of those options, what effect do they have on the risk? Do they eliminate the risk, reduce the risk to an acceptable level, or reduce the risk but the level of risk is still high?

What is the residual risk if these options are implemented? Is it low, medium or high?

As a result of these options, is the risk now acceptable?

Step 10: Sign off and record outcomes

Please note that if any items remain as 'High Risk' your **Data Protection Officer** (**DPO**) (or you if you don't have a **DPO**) must consult directly with the **Information Commissioner's Office** (**ICO**) before proceeding.

Are you happy to sign off any residual risk?

What does your **Data Protection Officer** (**DPO**) advise?

Have you accepted the **DPO** advice? If no, please document why and indicate who has made the decision to override the **DPO's** advice***

Add any additional comments

Set a date when this **DPIA** will next be reviewed.

*** If you are ever in the situation where you want to override the **DPO**'s advice, please think very carefully before you do so. If you go ahead and at a future date there is a problem with the process (maybe someone makes a **Data Subject Access Request** and then complains to the **ICO** about how their data is being processed by you), the **ICO** will look very closely into your operations if you have previously overridden advice from your **DPO**.

This is one of the reasons I am a strong advocate for organisations using external **DPO**s. The **DPO** has to be able to say "STOP – you are not processing data that way" if they feel there is a substantial risk to **Personally Identifiable Information**. If the **DPO** is a direct employee of your organisation they may well feel less able to do this, as directly or indirectly they may feel they are hampering their career progression. As an external **DPO**, I never have that concern, and therefore if I feel the risk is too high, I can, and have, said "STOP".

Fortunately, because many of my clients engage me early in the process, the number of occasions I have had to say STOP is less than the number of fingers on one hand. By working with your **DPO** early you can often ensure that the process plan is modified so that risk to **Personally Identifiable Information** is either eliminated or reduced to acceptable levels.

"I do" – the wonders of consent

I will discuss in the next chapter why it is not always necessary to gain a **Data Subject**'s express consent in order to hold their **personally identifiable information** (**PII**) or to process that data, but for the moment let's look at the key elements of consent.

Consent must be informed

Someone giving you consent must be fully aware what it is they are giving you consent for. Bear in mind that since the introduction of The Children's Code on 2nd September 2021, if your website is aimed at children, or could be used by children, then you may need Age-Appropriate privacy policies and wording around consent to ensure that the child can understand, just as easily as an adult, what it is they are giving you consent to do.

Consent must be manual

This essentially means that if you have a check box to indicate that the person completing the form is happy to give you their consent, this box should be blank and require a tick in the box (or a mouse click in the box) for the person to give their consent.

Consent must always be 'opt-in'

If we take marketing materials here as an example, your question seeking consent must say something along the lines of: -

I agree to you sending me marketing materials about your products and services.

You should not have a question along the lines of:

I understand that you will send me marketing materials about your products and services unless I tick this box to opt-out of such marketing.

It's a subtle difference, but an important difference. Don't be fooled by thinking that because some large retail websites still use the opt-out option it's ok to do so – it isn't.

Consent must explain why as well as what will be held

You need to explain what data you are going to hold about the person if they give their consent and what you are planning to do with that information once you have collected it. If you are planning to carry out any form of automated processing of the data, they are submitting you should say so.

In many cases, this will already be explained in your privacy policy, so provide a link to your privacy policy so people can easily access it. It is best practice to provide this link as close as possible to where you are asking them to tick the consent box – don't make them have to scroll all of the way to the bottom of your website to find it.

A note if you are collecting someone's consent in person, for example at a conference or trade show. It is very worthwhile to print out a copy (or copies) of your privacy policy and have these available for anyone to read on request.

While mentioning trade shows etc., this is one area where you need to be very careful that you are clearly telling people what you are going to do with their data.

To give you an example of this, let's say you have a bowl on your exhibition stand for people to throw their business cards into, and above that bowl you have a sign saying "Leave your business card here for the chance to win a new iPad"

Legally, all you can do with those business cards, is pick one out at the end of the day, dispatch the new iPad to the lucky winner and then throw all of the business cards into the shredder. Now, while if you are 100% altruistic that may have been your aim, for most people the aim will have been to add those people to your marketing list / contact list. That's perfectly fine *as long as you told the people leaving their cards that was what you were going to do with their information*. It's a simple change, just add the wording to the sign above the bowl, but make sure the wording is there or you could be building problems for the future.

Consent must explain how long data will be retained

As for the explanation of what you are going to do with the data, you need to let people know how long their data will be retained. Again, the easiest way of doing this may well be to give people easy access to your **privacy policy**.

Consent must be as easy to withdraw as it was to give

If all someone has to do to give you consent to contact them or store and process their data is to tick a box on a form, that must be all they need to do to remove their consent. For information on what you should and should not delete if they withdraw their consent, please see the "**The right to be forgotten**" chapter of this book.

If you deal with children (under 16) or the Data Subject is a vulnerable adult, consent must come from a parent or guardian

Since the introduction of The Children's Code on 2nd September 2021, young people under 16 cannot give their consent without you also gathering the consent of their parent or guardian.

There are two ways of dealing with this.

If you don't want to deal with people under the age of 16, simply add a tick box with wording "I confirm I am 16 years of age or older" to your consent form. If the young person lies about their age and ticks the box anyway then that is down to them, you have done what you need to do to try to prevent them accessing your products and/or services.

If you do want to deal with people under the age of 16, then you need to gain the consent of the parent or guardian (there are a few limited exceptions to this, for example where the child is reporting domestic abuse).

The established best practice way of doing this is to ask the young person to enter their parent or guardian's email address. Once you have that address, send an email to that address with a link within the email which when clicked will update the consent setting for the young person.

Of course, this solution is far from perfect, the young person may well know how to set up a new Gmail account, they then enter that email address as their parent or guardian's email address or their parent or guardian's mobile telephone number, and when they receive the confirmation email from your webserver, they of course click on the link to say they want the young person to be able to use your product or service. So yes, it has issues, but for now it is the best solution available to remain compliant.

Recording consent

It is important that if given online, your form records the date and time that consent is given, and it is also best practice to record the IP address used to submit the form.

If you gather information physically, for example at a trade show, at the minimum record the date that consent is given, and preferably record the date and time.

What about business cards?

If you meet someone and they give you their business card, they are giving you *implied consent* to contact them once. So, you can follow up on the business card, but you must give them the option to say, "Please don't contact me anymore".

What if I have a lead magnet (or giveaway), I want to ensure the person completing the form gives me consent before I give my lead magnet away?

Unfortunately, you can't do this. If your form advertises a free item, for example a free checklist or maybe admission to a webinar, you must still give the person completing the form the items you are advertising even if they don't give you, their consent.

Now, you might be thinking, well how can I do that, if I'm not allowed to store their contact information. Well, you can use the data to send them whatever the giveaway is, but you then must immediately delete their data.

A quick note about employees and consent.

Legal precedent has established that an employee can never give you consent (which is why you would rely on the contractual legal basis for storing and processing your employee data).

Why can't an employee give you consent? Because the law states that consent must be freely given. It has been argued that an employee could consider that not giving consent could have a negative impact on their future employment with your organisation and therefore they could feel under duress to give you consent.

Do I always need consent to process data?

This is perhaps one of the most misunderstood concepts of GDPR. If I had a pound for every time someone has told me "Oh, we had lots of contact details of business prospects but we didn't had consent so we had to throw it away when GDPR came in", I would have my own yacht on the Mediterranean by now.

Let's be clear – consent is **the** platinum standard, if you can gain someone's consent, then you probably should, but not having someone's consent does not necessarily stop you from using their data for marketing or other purposes.

One reason to be cautious of seeking someone's consent, even if you can seek it, is that the rules of GDPR is very clear, if someone has given you their consent to use their data for a particular purpose, it must be just as simple for them to retract their consent – so if you've asked them to tick a box on a web form to give you consent, all they need to do to remove that consent is untick a box on a web form, and as soon as they do, that's it, you can't use their data for that purpose any more.

Consider that for a moment – a potential client gives you their express consent to market to them, you spend two years (with all the associated expense) sending them marketing materials and then suddenly one day, with no warning to you, that potential client withdraws their consent. That's game over, from that moment you can no longer market to them….

So, if you don't always need to have consent to use someone's personally identifiable information, what other reasons can you rely on?

Contractual

If you have a contract with someone, whether that is as an employee, client, supplier etc. you don't need to also seek consent in order to contact them. However, do so with care, your communication must be what a reasonable person would consider to be appropriate. So, to give you an example, if you sold someone a bicycle, you could legitimately contact them about bicycles or bicycle helmets or bicycle accessories. What you couldn't do without gaining their additional consent would be to suddenly start sending them marketing material about microwave ovens.

Legal Obligation

You don't need someone's consent to hold their information where you have a legal obligation to do so. Typically, this will be employee payroll information or client sales information, both of which you have to retain because Her Majesty's Revenue and Customs has written into law that you must do so.

Vital Interests

For most people, vital interests will be the legal basis relied on by the National Health Service for retaining your medical data. Outside of a healthcare environment, this is a trickier one to use, but an example would be for instance if you had an employee who was diabetic or epileptic, you could use vital interests as a reason to retain that information on their employee records, so that should they have an episode while at work, you could provide the appropriate information to any paramedics.

Public Task

This reason can really only be relied on by Government bodies, whether that is Central Government, County Councils or Unitary Authorities, Borough or District Councils and Parish Councils.

Legitimate Interests

This is perhaps the most common reason for retaining and processing someone's data without their express consent. If you can justify holding that person's data on the basis that your organisation requires that data to perform its normal functions, then you can use legitimate interests to retain that data.

At first, this might appear a perfect cop-out. Why not just use legitimate interest to store all **personally identifiable information (PII)**?

The answer is because you may be asked to justify it in a court of law. That means that if you have not carried out a **Data Privacy Impact Assessment (DPIA)** and clearly documented how you concluded that retaining each field of information was in your legitimate interest, you will almost certainly find yourself facing a penalty from the **ICO** (and potentially a claim for damages from the **Data Subject**).

So, if you are relying on legitimate interest for any personally identifiable information, make sure you have conducted a **Data Privacy Impact Assessment**. Fortunately, we tell you exactly how to do this in the **Complete a Data Privacy Impact Assessment** chapter of this book.

Dealing with Data Subject Access Requests

The first thing to realise is that a **Data Subject Access Request** (**DSAR**) can come from absolutely anyone, your users, employees, clients, suppliers or even just a random member of the public.

The second thing to realise is that a **Data Subject Access Request** can be made either in writing or verbally, and as far as GDPR and UK GDPR are concerned, both are equally valid.

You may well have a form which you like people to complete when they make a **Data Subject Access Request**. While this is very useful for you, you can't make it compulsory, if someone makes the request over the telephone to you, or in a WhatsApp chat, all are equally valid.

However, the request is made, it is crucially important that you record the date and time that the request is received, as you have 30 days from the date of the request to get the requested information back to the person who made the request.

So, now you have got the **Data Subject Access Request** what do you do next?

I recommend three things: -

1) don't panic – you do only have 30 days but that is plenty of time if you handle the request correctly

2) write to the person to request that they confirm who they say they are – you don't want to send the information to anyone other than the Data Subject or

their appointed representative, that if it happens, would be a Data Breach.

3) While you are writing to the person, try to get them to be more specific about what information they are asking for. Explain that by being more specific, it will increase the chance of the information you supply satisfying their request.

In reality of course, what you are doing with item 3 is reducing the amount of work that you need to do. While some people will put in a request that they want 'absolutely everything', my experience has shown that is very much the exception rather than the rule. In general, if you write and ask someone to be more specific (and you ensure your request is polite and respectful), the **Data Subject** will refine their request. So, it may reduce from 'everything' to 'all emails between themselves and the organisation and any internal emails within the organisation that mention them, within the last 6 months – a much easier request to satisfy.

Dealing with **Data Subject Access Requests** is another reason for having a really clear **Data Retention Policy**. If the **Data Subject** has asked for all emails that have mentioned them in the last 10 years, and your **Data Retention Policy** states that you only retain customer emails for 6 months, then you can send them emails from the last 6 months, together with a copy of your **Data Retention Policy** and explain that in line with the policy, any emails older than 6 months simply no longer exist and therefore it is not possible to provide them.

I will add a note of caution here though a) be certain that your **Data Retention Policy** is *actually being followed* and b) be prepared to *demonstrate that it is being followed*. If you don't, and an email older than 6 months suddenly appears, you could find yourself facing a claim for damages from the **Data Subject**.

I've mentioned the 30-day limit for responding to **Data Subject Access Requests**. Due to this time limit I would advise you that as soon as the **Data Subject** has clarified their request (or from the date of the original request if the request was suitably specific) you begin to gather the data to send to the **Data Subject**. Don't wait for the Data Subject to confirm who they are, that can wait, it is not a reason not to start gathering the information together – I will explain why in a moment.

How should I check that the Data Subject Access Request is genuine?

This varies depending on whether the **Data Subject** has applied to you directly or whether the request has come from a solicitor or other person acting on the **Data Subject**'s behalf.

For both scenarios you should ask for one piece of photo ID (i.e., a copy of a passport or driving licence) and one piece of ID to confirm the **Data Subject**'s address (for example, a recent utility bill).

In the case where the request has come from a solicitor or other agent acting on the **Data Subject**'s behalf, you should also ask for a signed letter to you from the applicant, stating the solicitor or agent's name and that they authorise you to produce their information direct to the solicitor or agent.

The reason I say you should continue sourcing the data to satisfy the **Data Subject Access Request** is that some people, and in particular some solicitors, know that you only have 30 days from the date of the original request to produce the data. They will therefore delay providing you with confirmation of their identity until day 28 or 29 in the hope that will mean that they will prevent you from satisfying the **Data Subject Access Request** and as a result, then pursuing a claim against you for non-material damages for their client, to compensate their client for the distress you have caused them by not being able to release all of their data in time.

Should I release the data to the Data Subject before I have confirmed their identity (and/or their consent for the agent to act on their behalf)?

Absolutely not. If you were to issue someone's data to the wrong person that would be a **Data Breach**. If you are not confident of the identity of the **Data Subject**, do not release the data.

What format should I release the data to the Data Subject in?

Unless they have requested an alternative, simply provide the information in textual form via an email or postal letter.

I would recommend you provide all of the information in **PDF** format if sending it electronically.

This is one instance where sometimes postal mail can be an advantage over email as you can send it by Recorded Delivery or Special Delivery, and someone will need to sign for it (either the **Data Subject** or someone acting on their behalf). Because Royal Mail will record the date and time the delivery took place, you have verifiable proof that you satisfied the **Data Subject Access Request** within the time allowed, should it ever be queried later.

If the data requested includes video footage (for example **CCTV** footage), I would not recommend that you provide the **Data Subject** with a copy of the footage (as you don't know how it may be manipulated by the **Data Subject**). Instead, I would recommend that you upload the footage to your web server (or ask your web developer to do this if you don't know how to do it yourself), and then simply provide a **URL** to the **Data Subject** and tell them that by going to that **URL** they can view the footage. You may also wish to put a time limit on the viewing, i.e., make it available for viewing for 7 days or 30 days as appropriate.

Do I need to edit any of the information before I send it?

Yes, you should read through all of the information and ensure you redact the names and email addresses of anyone who is not the **Data Subject**. The **Data Subject** has no right to see these other names and emails and to release them to the **Data Subject** is potentially a **Data Breach**.

This is also why I recommend sending the data either as **PDF** files or as physical printed documents. Either of these approaches minimises the opportunity for the **Data Subject** to remove any redaction, whereas if you send the documents as Word or Excel documents, it is relatively easy for the **Data Subject** to remove redaction and gain access to information they are not entitled to see.

If the **Data Subject** has requested any photographs or video footage you may need to get them professionally edited before being sent to the **Data Subject**. If the images contain faces of anybody other than the **Data Subject**, you will need to redact those faces. Equally you should redact the number plates of any vehicles in the photos or video footage unless the vehicle concerned is owned by the applicant. If you need any help with this, please check out the **Useful Resources** towards the back of this book.

What if there is so much information, I simply can't compile it all and get it to the Data Subject within 30 days?

If you become aware that for reason of the sheer volume of data, or for some other reason you are not going to be able to meet the 30 day deadline you have two options.

Either a) write to the **Data Subject** at the earliest opportunity and let them know you need more time, and explain why **or**

b) wait until you are almost at the 30 day deadline, send the **Data Subject** all of the information you have collated up to that point and tell them that you need more time to provide the rest of the information, and explain why.

You should use this provision as rarely as possible, do not allow it to become your standard response. Why? Because if you take more than 30 days to provide all of the information, the **Data Subject** can ask the **ICO** to question why you needed the extra time. If the **ICO** is not satisfied with your reasoning, they may impose a financial penalty.

The Data Subject has told me that English is not their first language, and so can I provide all of the information in Italian?

While you can do this if you wish, you are under absolutely no legal obligation to do so. As long as you provide the information in English, it is up to the **Data Subject** to arrange translation if required.

Should I record on the Data Subject's record that I have provided them with information in response to a Data Subject Access Request?

Definitely yes. You should record the date and time that you provided the information. The reason for this is a) it helps to determine if someone is making regular repeated requests; and b) if that **Data Subject** makes another request 6 months after the initial request, you are only required to provide them with anything that has changed or been updated since their previous request. If they've lost what you originally sent them, that is their problem, and you can make a charge to them if they ask you to provide the information again.

Can I charge the Data Subject for complying with the Data Subject Access Request?

In most cases, no you can't make a charge. The exception is if the **Data Subject** makes requests too often (for example more than once every three calendar months), or that the request is clearly vexatious (i.e., you can prove that you have never conducted any business with the **Data Subject**).

In either of these cases you are allowed to make a 'reasonable charge' for provision of the data, which has been established by precedent to be £10 per hour multiplied by the number of hours it has taken to collate the data – so if it has taken you 40 hours and the **Data Subject Access Request** is either too frequent or vexatious, then you can charge the **Data Subject** £400 for providing the information. This can be very useful if the **Data Subject** informs you, they have lost the data you sent them and asks you to send it again.

So, what happens after you've satisfied a Data Subject Access Request?

In most cases, nothing at all.

However, the **Data Subject**, having received their **Personally Identifiable Information** (**PII**) after submitting a **Data Subject Access Request** (**DSAR**) can do one of the following: -

They can request a breakdown and explanation of how any profiling or automatic processing has been carried out (see the **AI AI** chapter of this book) or they can ask for any errors in their data to be corrected.

If they do ask for corrections to their data, you should make these corrections (or provide them with a written explanation of why the corrections cannot be made) within 30 days of receipt of the request.

Once the corrections are completed, you should write to the **Data Subject** to confirm that the corrections have been made. It is possible at this point that the **Data Subject** will make a further **Data Subject Access Request** to enable them to verify that all of the changes have been made. You should comply with this **Data Subject Access Request** and should not normally charge for doing so.

The **Data Subject** may also question whether you really have provided all of the information you hold about them. If you receive such a question, you should consider whether you need to conduct another trawl through all of the data relating to the **Data Subject** to see if you have missed something, or you can go back to the **Data Subject** to get more details of what they feel is missing. If you are confident that you do not have that information, for example because it has been destroyed in line with your **Data Retention Policy** (see the **Creating a Data Retention Policy** chapter of this book for more details), then you should simply write back to the **Data Subject** to explain that this is the case.

The Right to be Forgotten

Other than consent, the right to be forgotten is perhaps one of the most misunderstood concepts under GDPR.

I think in some ways this is due to the wording, it would have been better if the wording had said "The Right to ASK to be Forgotten" as that would be a clearer indication of what it means.

Everyone has the 'Right to be Forgotten' under GDPR, but if someone contacts you and asks to execute their right to be forgotten, there are all sorts of reasons why you may turn around and say "No, sorry, we can't forget you."

So, let's look at a few of those reasons:

If the law says that you need to retain their records, you can't forget them – an example would be where you have an invoice to record a sale made to them, or they have been an employee of yours within the last 6 years so Her Majesty's Revenue and Customs (HMRC) say you must keep their payroll records.

If you need their personal information because you need it to fulfil a contract with them – examples here would be because they were an employee of yours, or they are a customer with an ongoing maintenance contract, or they are a customer and not all of the items they have ordered have yet been supplied to them.

Where you have CCTV records of them, and you believe they may have committed a criminal act while on your premises.

Where you have reasonable reason to believe that there may be a civil 'class' action in the future. An example could be where they have sampled a cosmetics product and you are aware through the industry press that there has been legal action concerning one of the ingredients either within the UK or overseas.

However, I should add a couple of notes of caution:

It may be that in some cases, you are able to delete some of the information you hold about someone, but not all of it.

Typically this will be the case with ex-employees. While you can justify retaining their payroll records (because the law says you must) and you might want to retain their past 3-year annual appraisals (and if you dismissed the employee, you may well want to keep records of the disciplinary process), you could not justify retaining annual appraisals from ten years ago or what the employee's meal choices had been for the last company Christmas lunch.

Whatever you decide, it is important that within 30 days of receiving the request to be forgotten, you write back to the individual involved and tell them what categories of data you have deleted, and what categories of data you have retained (and why you have retained them).

AI AI?

GDPR and UK GDPR provide that any processing of **Personally Identifiable Information** (**PII**) via automated profiling or decision-making cannot be fully automatic – there has to be a human review at some stage during the process.

If you perform any kind of automated profiling or decision making on **Personally Identifiable Information** (**PII**) and you have provided some of this data to a **Data Subject** in response to a **Data Subject Access Request**, the **Data Subject** can ask you for a breakdown of how the profiling or decision-making works.

If you receive such a request, you again have 30 days from the date of the request to provide the **Data Subject** with a written description of the processing, detailing each step of the process, what happens to the data, and how the profiling or decision making is performed.

This is a good example of where creating **Data Privacy Impact Assessments** for each of the key elements of your data processing within your organisation can prove long term to be a great timesaver and so a great investment. Why? Because if your **Data Privacy Impact Assessment** has been done correctly, this description of the processing will have already been written and it will be a simple copy and paste operation to send this information to the **Data Subject**.

If you hadn't previously carried out a **Data Privacy Impact Assessment** for the process(es) involved, now would be a good time to do them. Although it may take several hours work to do, it really is a case of do it once, benefit many times, so it is well worth the effort. Otherwise, you end up detailing the process every time you receive a query in response to a **Data Subject Access Request**, and it's really not worth the aggravation.

The Right to Stop Processing

Typically, although not exclusively, this will occur after a **Data Subject Access Request** and the **Data Subject** concerned has spotted some processing of their data that they are not happy with you performing.

Data Subjects may access this right in one of two ways, either they can say please stop automated processing of my data or please stop all processing of my data.

Let's look at a real example of a **Data Subject** using their rights under the provision of **The Right to Stop Processing,** which happened to one of my clients.

An employee who had only been with the company for a few months submitted a **Data Subject Access Request** and was quite specific in that they asked for details of how the company processed their payroll.

The company provided the information requested in the **Data Subject Access Request**, and having had an opportunity to review the contents, the employee made a request via **The Right to Stop Processing**.

The issue was that my client was using a **Data Processor**, let's call them Acme Payroll Services, to process all of the company's payroll. The **Data Subject** in this case, had a bad experience with Acme Payroll Services in the past, and so submitted a request via **The Right to Stop Processing** requesting that his payroll was no longer processed by Acme Payroll Services.

My client was happy with the services provided by Acme Payroll Services and did not wish to stop using them for the company payroll, however, they now had to find a way of processing this particular **Data Subject**'s payroll. They did not have anyone in-house who could process a payroll, and they had no desire to train someone to do so, so instead they contracted a different payroll agency, let's call them XYZ Payroll Services just to run the payroll for the **Data Subject**. Although there was added cost in doing this, they reasoned that at least now they were using two payroll services, if another of their employees made a request for them to stop using Acme Payroll Services, and/or they had a contractual issue with Acme Payroll Services, at least they would now have an alternative payroll provider (XYZ Payroll Services) that they already had a relationship with and so they could transfer the whole payroll to XYZ Payroll Services with minimal disruption.

On the face of it, for companies and other organisations, **Data Subjects** having this right can seem a scary subject. In reality, don't worry about it too much, requests to stop processing are relatively rare, across my 150+ clients only 2 requests to stop processing have been received in just over 3 years, and with a combined total of well over 1 million **Data Subjects** within those clients, you can hopefully see that the chance of you receiving a request to stop processing is a rare event.

Just what is a Data Breach?

If I were to ask you to tell me what a **Data Breach** was under **GDPR**, my guess is that the first thing that comes to mind is your organisation's database being hacked by bad actors, or an employee accessing data which they weren't authorised to access.

While both of those are certainly **Data Breaches**, they are far from the only possible causes of a **Data Breach**.

Before we move on to looking at how you deal with a **Data Breach**, let's firstly consider some other scenarios which can result in a **Data Breach**: -

Leaving your laptop, tablet, or mobile phone on the train or on the bus

This in itself is a **Data Breach** and should be recorded in your **Data Breach Register**.

Putting the wrong invoice in the wrong envelope (or indeed putting the wrong pay slip in the wrong envelope)

Both of these are **Data Breaches** and should be recorded in your **Data Breach Register**.

They are a **Data Breach** because someone other than the intended recipient now knows how much someone owes you (in the case of an invoice) or how much someone else at your organisation gets paid (in the case of a pays lip).

In both of these cases you should ask the recipient to either return the document to you or to confirm that they have destroyed the document.

Sending information as an attachment or within the body of an email to the wrong person

In my experience, this is the second most common **Data Breach** I come across amongst my clients. It is so easy to do and most of us if we are honest will probably confess to having done it ourselves at least once. (Confession time, I actually did this myself last week!)

As for the other breaches, the first action should be to record the **Data Breach** in your **Data Breach Register**.

As per the previous example, you should also contact the person you send the wrong information too and ask them to delete the original email and/or attachments.

Using cc in email with external email addresses instead of bcc

This is by far the most common **Data Breach** I come across with my clients. If you put an external email address into the CC field of an email, and the owner of that email address has not given you express permission to do so, you've caused a **Data Breach**.

Again, just record that it has happened in the **Data Breach Register**. And next time, remember to use BCC instead of CC, it really only takes a little while for it to become a new habit.

It is important that you understand why this is a **Data Breach** and what you should do about it. HIV Scotland didn't and in September 2021 they got fined £10,000 by the **ICO** exactly for this **Data Breach** and not recording it in their **Data Breach Register**.

Not being sufficiently careful with confidential waste

OK, for the first time in this book, I'm going to get on my soapbox on this one. Confidential Waste is confidential, right? – so don't have a great big bright yellow bin behind your reception desk with Confidential Waste written on it in

6-inch-high letters. OK – so I'm exaggerating a bit, but I'm sure you have all seen examples of what I mean.

Please don't do it, especially behind reception and along corridors. To bad actors, confidential waste bins are like a proverbial honeypot, they will gladly swipe everything that's in them in the hope they can seize something of value. So keep it all subtle. You know which bin it is you don't need to advertise it to the world.

In the event confidential waste does go missing, you know the drill by now, enter the details into your **Data Breach Register**. However, in this instance, depending on what you think was in the waste gone missing and how many people could be affected, you need to consider also reporting the **Data Breach** to the **Information Commissioner's Office**.

The other thing to be careful of is if you are still using an old-style 'Spaghetti' shredder to shred documents. If you are using this outdated equipment, please stop using it as soon as possible and invest in a new crosscut shredder (details of some suitable shredders are included in the **Useful Resources** chapter of this book).

The reason spaghetti shredders are now strongly discouraged is that however much you mix up the paper strips, there are people with sad enough lives that armed with their trusty roll of sellotape they will take the strips and seek to reassemble them into sheets of paper so they can extract the data for their own uses.

Having too much information in your Visitor's book and having it too clearly accessible

Ensure your visitor's book collects the minimum amount of data required – ok you need to know the visitor's name and who they are seeing, you need to know their vehicle registration number if they are parked in your car park, but do you really need to know which company they are from or what their mobile telephone number is? If the answer is no, stop collecting these details in your visitor's book.

I've included details of some good **UK GDPR** compliant visitor's books in the **Useful Resources** chapter of this book

Data displayed on the receptionist's screen which is visible to people standing at reception

There are two ways around this one, the first is to change where the screen is located to make it much more difficult to see the screen from where visitors stand. The second if that does not achieve the desired result is to add a filter to the front of the monitor causing the problem. The filter narrows down the viewing angle of the screen. Again, I've put a link to suitable screens in the **Useful Resources** chapter of this book.

Putting a letter of appreciation up on the staff noticeboard without redacting the address and signature.

We all like receiving praise for our work, but if you receive a thankyou letter from one of your clients, or perhaps from a member of staff who has gone on maternity leave, and you want to put the letter on display, there is no problem with doing so, just make sure you have redacted the address etc. and signature first.

Dealing with a Data Breach

In the last chapter, I detailed what a **Data Breach** actually is. Now, let's look at how to deal with them.

The first thing to do, however small the **Data Breach** is record the **Data Breach** in your **Data Breach Register**. Depending on how your organisation is set up you might do this yourself, or by notifying your **Data Protection Officer** (**DPO**) or your **External Data Protection Officer** (**DPO**).

Your **Data Breach Register** is, after your **Privacy Policy**, the most important document in your **GDPR / UK GDPR** documentation.

The **Data Breach Register** itself does not have to be a complicated document. It can be as simple as an Excel spreadsheet. You can access a **Data Breach Register** template via the URL in the **Useful Resources** section of this book.

You and your employees should look on the **Data Breach Register** just as you do your company Accident Book. You wouldn't discipline a staff member for cutting their finger three times in a month and entering those events in your Accident Book. In the same way you should encourage your staff to enter all **Data Breaches**, however small, into your **Data Breach Register**. As per the Accident Book, these entries should not be used to discipline staff, but they can be very useful in identifying where your training resources are best directed.

Having recorded the incident in your **Data Breach Register**, you then need to decide whether any further action is necessary, and if further action is required, should it go as far as notifying the **ICO** of the **Data Breach**.

Obviously, if the **Data Breach** was really simple (such as sending the wrong invoice in the wrong envelope), the only action required would be to contact the client who received the wrong invoice, ask them to either return that invoice or confirm that they have destroyed it, and issue the client with the correct invoice.

If the **Data Breach** is more complicated than that, and typically will therefore involve electronic data, then the decision on what to do next depends on the potential harm to **Data Subjects** and the number of **Data Subjects** affected.

There is no hard and fast rule on when either the potential harm or number of **Data Subjects** is sufficient that the **Data Breach** needs to be escalated to the **ICO**. I have put a couple of examples below, but please remember that each case must be considered on its merits.

Example 1 is where a member of staff has emailed a sales promotion to 10 of your clients and has accidentally used the cc field to send the email rather than bcc.

The only **Personally Identifiable Information** involved in this data breach are email addresses and, in some cases, people's names.

Given that the number of people affected is relatively low, and the only data exposed is email addresses, my advice would be that this incident would not need reporting to the **ICO**.

What would need to happen is to issue a second email to each of the recipients of the first email (this time not using the cc field!) and ask them to delete the original email.

This action AND how we came to the conclusion not to escalate to the **ICO** should be recorded in your **Data Breach Register**.

Example 2 begins with your IT Department notifying you that overnight your IT system has been hacked. While they are confident that they have now patched the system and it can no longer be infiltrated using the method used by the perpetrators overnight, they have studied your server logs and are as confident as they can be that all of the payroll data of your 250 employees has been extracted. They are still investigating but believe that a file containing full names, home addresses, mobile phone numbers, email addresses, passwords, salary and payslip information, and sickness leave information has been taken.

Given the number of people affected and the sensitive nature of some of the data believed to have been stolen, my advice would be that this incident does need escalating through the full **Data Breach** escalation process, culminating in notification to the **Information Commissioner's Office** (**ICO**). I'm going to lead you step by step through that process now.

Once you have entered the **Data Breach** into your **Data Breach Register**, the next thing I would say is "don't panic!" You have 72 hours from when the **Data Breach** *occurs* or from when you first became aware of the **Data Breach** (which depending on the timing of the breach and its complexity could be hours, days or even weeks after the **Data Breach** originally occurred).

For the next steps, the flow chart on the next page will probably be useful. I have also included this flow chart in the files available for download via the link in the **Useful Resources** section of this book. You might find it useful to go there, download the flow chart and print it out to have it easily accessible while you progress through the rest of this chapter.

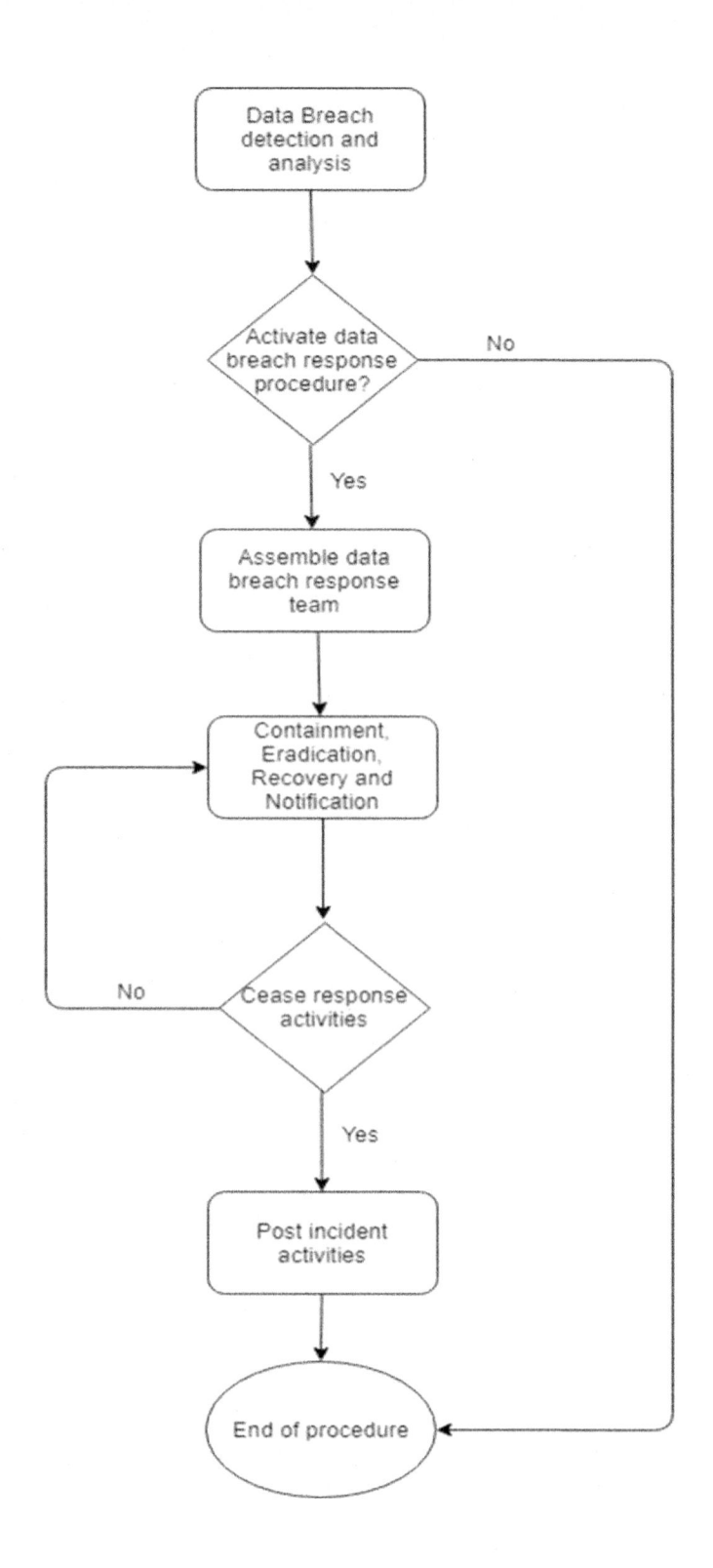

```
┌─────────────────┐
│ Data Breach     │
│ detection and   │
│ analysis        │
└────────┬────────┘
         │
         ▼
      ◇ Activate data ◇ ─── No ───┐
      ◇ breach response ◇          │
      ◇ procedure?    ◇            │
         │                         │
        Yes                        │
         ▼                         │
┌─────────────────┐                │
│ Assemble data   │                │
│ breach response │                │
│ team            │                │
└────────┬────────┘                │
         │                         │
         ▼                         │
┌─────────────────┐                │
│ Containment,    │◄───┐           │
│ Eradication,    │    │           │
│ Recovery and    │    │           │
│ Notification    │    │           │
└────────┬────────┘    │           │
         │             │           │
         ▼             │           │
   ◇ Cease response ◇ ─No─┘        │
   ◇ activities    ◇               │
         │                         │
        Yes                        │
         ▼                         │
┌─────────────────┐                │
│ Post incident   │                │
│ activities      │                │
└────────┬────────┘                │
         │                         │
         ▼                         │
     ( End of procedure )◄─────────┘
```

84

Data Breach Team
In the following pages I will describe several roles to be performed by various members of your **Data Breach Team**. I recognise that depending upon the size of your organisation, one person may have to adopt more than one of the roles (or indeed quite possibly all of the roles if you are an organisation with less than 3 – 4 people).

Activating the Data Breach procedure

You should nominate a **Data Breach** team leader for controlling the response to this **Data Breach**.

The **Data Breach** team leader will normally be your **Data Protection Officer** (**DPO**) if you have one. If you don't have one or they are unavailable, then a member of your management team should assume the **Data Breach** team leader role.

The **Data Breach** team leader should satisfy themselves that a full **Data Breach Team** response is required.

I would normally recommend you take the following into account when trying to decide:
- Is there significant actual or potential loss of sensitive information?
- Is there significant actual or potential disruption to normal business operation?
- Are there significant risks to business reputation?
- Is this another situation which may cause significant impact to the organisation?

in the event of disagreement or uncertainty about whether or not to activate the **Data Breach Team** procedure, the decision of the **Data Breach** team leader shall be final.

If it is decided not to activate the procedure, a plan should be created to allow for a lower-level response to the **Data Breach** and the decision recorded in your **Data Breach Register**.

If the **Data Breach Team** leader is satisfied that the incident warrants the activation of the **Data Breach Team** procedure, the **Data Breach Team** leader will start to assemble the **Data Breach Team**.

The **Data Breach Team** will consist of the following roles: Team leader, Team facilitator, Incident Liaison, Information Technology, Business Operations, Facilities Management, Health and Safety, Human Resources, Business Continuity Planning, Communications (PR and social media), your **Data Protection Officer** and/or **external Data Protection Officer**.

The responsibilities of each of these roles is given below:

Team Leader

- decide whether or not to initiate a response
- assembles the **Data Breach Response Team**
- overall management of the **Data Breach Response Team**
- acts as the interface with the board and other high-level stakeholders
- final decision maker in case of any disagreement

Team Facilitator

- supports the **Data Breach Response Team**
- coordinate resources within the command centre
- prepares for meetings and takes record of actions and decisions
- brief team members on latest status on their return to the command centre
- facilitates communication by email, telephone or other methods
- monitors external information feeds such as news and social media

Incident Liaison

- attends the site of the incident as quickly as possible
- assesses the extent and impact of the incident
- provides first person account of the situation to the **Data Breach Team** leader
- liaises with the **Data Breach Team** leader on an ongoing basis to provide updates and answer any questions required for decision-making by the **Data Breach Response Team**

Information Technology

- provide input on technology-related issues
- assists with impact assessment

Business Operations

- contribute to decision-making based on knowledge of business operations, products and services
- briefs other members of the data breach team on operational issues
- helps to assess the likely impact on customers or employees of the organisation

Facilities Management

- deals with aspects of physical security and access
- provide security presence if required

Health and Safety

- assesses the risk to life and limb of the incident
- ensures that the legal responsibilities for health and safety are met at all times
- liaises with emergency services such as police, fire and ambulance
- considers environmental issues with respect to the incident

Human Resources

- assesses and advises on HR policy and employment contract matters
- represents the interests of the organisation's employees
- advises on capability and disciplinary issues

Business Continuity Planning

- provide advice on business continuity options
- invoke business continuity plans if required

Communications (PR and Social Media)

- responsible for ensuring internal communication is effective
- decide the level, frequency and content communication with external parties such as the media
- defined approach to keeping affected parties informed, e.g. customers, clients, suppliers, business partners, shareholders

Data Protection Officer

- advises on what must be done to ensure compliance with relevant laws and regulatory frameworks
- assesses the actual and potential legal implications of the incident and subsequent actions

As I said a few pages ago, I recognise that depending upon the size of your organisation, one person may have to adopt more than one of the roles (or indeed quite possibly all of the roles if you are an organisation with less than 3 – 4 people).

The **Data Breach Team** leader will ensure that all team members (or their deputies, if main team members are uncontactable) are contacted, made aware of the nature of the **Data Breach** and asked to assemble at an appropriate location or given the access details for a virtual meeting using Zoom, Microsoft Teams or similar virtual meeting solutions.

The Incident Liaison will be asked to attend the location of the incident (if not at the company premises) in order to start to gather information for the **Data Breach** assessment that the **Data Breach** team will conduct so that an appropriate response can be determined.

If the **Data Breach** has occurred at one of your **Data Processors**, the Incident Liaison should be a member of the senior management team at the **Data Processor**.

Once an appropriate response to the **Data Breach** has been identified, the **Data Breach Response Team** needs to be able to manage the overall response, monitor the status of the incident and ensure effective communication is taking place at all levels within the company.

Regular **Data Breach Response Team** meetings must be held at an appropriate frequency as decided by the **Data Breach Team** leader. A standard agenda for these meetings can be downloaded via the URL in the **Useful Resources** section of this book. The purpose of these meetings is to ensure that **Data Breach** management resources are managed effectively and that decisions are made promptly based on adequate information. Each meeting will be minuted by the Team Facilitator.

The **Data Breach** liaison will provide updates to the **Data Breach Response Team** at a frequency decided by the **Data Breach Response Team** leader. These updates should be coordinated with the **Data Breach Response Team** meetings so that the latest information is always available for each meeting.

It is vital that effective communications are maintained between all parties involved in the **Data Breach** response.

The primary means of communication during an incident will initially be face-to-face and telephone, both landline and mobile. Email should not be used unless everyone is satisfied that the email system itself has not been breached and permission to use email has been given by the **Data Breach Response Team**.

The following guidelines should be followed into all communications:

- be calm and avoid lengthy conversation
- advise internal team members of the need to refer information requests to the **Data Breach Response Team**
- if a call from media, or someone else outside of the organisation, is received by someone other than the person appointed to deal with communications, the person taking the call should ask for contact details of the caller and pass them on to the appropriate person as soon as possible. No one, other than those appointed by the **Data Breach Response Team**, should speak to those outside the organisation, especially to the media or to clients.
- always document call time details, responses and actions

All communications should be clearly and accurately recorded as records may be needed as part of legal action at a later date.

Depending on the nature of the **Data Breach** there may be a variety of external parties that will need to be communicated with during the course of the **Data Breach** response. It is important that the information released to 3rd parties is managed so that it is both timely and accurate.

Calls that are not from agencies directly involved with the **Data Breach** response (such as the media) should be passed to the member of the **Data Breach Response Team** responsible for communications.

There may be a number of external parties who, while not directly involved in the incident, may be affected by it and need to be alerted to the incident. These may include:

- customers
- suppliers
- employees
- regulatory bodies
- shareholders

The Communications **Data Breach Response Team** member should make a list of such interested parties and define the message that is to be given to them. The formulation of this message may involve communication with senior management of the company and with any external agencies.

Interested parties who have not been alerted by the **Data Breach Response Team** may call to obtain information about the incident and its effects. These calls should be recorded in the message log and passed to the appointed Communications member of the **Data Breach Response Team**.

In general, the communication strategy with respect to the media will be to issue updates via senior management. No members of staff should give an interview to the media unless this has been pre-authorised by senior management and the **Data Breach Response Team**.

The preferred method to interface with the media will be to issue prewritten press releases. In exceptional circumstances a press conference will be held to answer questions about the incident and its effect on clients and employees. It is the responsibility of the communications **Data Breach Response Team** member to arrange a venue for these and to liaise with any press who may wish to attend.

In drafting a statement for the media the following guidelines should be observed:

- personal information should be protected at all times

- stick to the facts and do not speculate about the incident or its cause
- ensure legal advice is obtained prior to any statements suggesting criminal activity being issued
- try to pre-empt questions that may reasonably be asked and provide answers for these as part of the media release
- emphasise that prepared response is been activated and that everything possible is being done to resolve the **Data Breach** as quickly as possible

The most appropriate spokesperson will depend upon the style of the incident and its effect upon customers, employees, suppliers, other stakeholders and the wider public.

Incident Containment

The next step will be to try to stop the incident getting any worse, i.e. to contain it. In the case of a virus outbreak or malware infection this may entail disconnecting the affected parts of the network; for a hacking attack, it may involve disabling certain profiles or ports on the firewall or perhaps even disconnecting the internal network from the Internet altogether. The specific actions to be performed will depend on the individual circumstances of each data breach.

Note: if it is judged to be likely that digital evidence will need to be collected that will later be used in court, precautions must be taken to ensure that such evidence remains admissible. This means that the relevant data must not be changed either deliberately or by accident. It is recommended that specialist advice should be obtained at this point.

Particularly (but not exclusively) if foul play is suspected in the incident, accurate records must be kept of the actions taken and the evidence gathered in line with digital forensic guidelines. The main principles of these guidelines as follows:

Principle 1 - don't change any data. If anything is done, and the data on the relevant system is altered in any way, then this may affect any subsequent court case.

Principle 2 - only access the original data in exceptional circumstances. A trained specialist will use tools to take a bit copy of any data held in memory, whether it's on a hard drive, flash memory or Sim card on a phone. All analysis will then take place on the copy and the original should never be touched unless in exceptional circumstances, e.g., time is of the essence and gaining information to prevent a further crime is more important than keeping the original evidence.

Principle 3 - always keep an audit trail what's been done. Forensic tools will do this automatically, but this also applies to the accident of the first people on the scene. Taking photographs and videos is encouraged, providing that this does not itself compromise any data.

Principle 4 - the person in charge must ensure that these guidelines are followed.

Prior to the arrival of a specialist, basic information should be collected. This may include:

- photographs or videos of relevant message or information
- manual written records of the chronology of the incident
- original documents, including records of who found them, where and when
- details of any witnesses

Once collected, the evidence will be kept in a safe place where it cannot be tampered with.

The evidence may be required:

- for later analysis as to the cause of the incident
- as forensic evidence for criminal or civil court proceedings

- in any compensation negotiations with software or service providers

Next, a clear picture of what happened needs to be established. The extent of the incident and any knock-on implications should be ascertained as soon as possible.

You may need your IT specialist to examine computer audit logs to piece together the sequence of events; care should be taken that only secure copies of logs which have not been tampered with are used.

Incident eradication

Actions to fix the damage caused by the incident, such as removing malware, must be put through your normal change management process (as an emergency change if necessary). These actions should be aimed at fixing the current cause and preventing any similar incident re-occurring. Any vulnerabilities that have been exploited as part the incident should be identified.

Depending on the type of incident, restoring data from a backup may be necessary.

Recovery

During the recovery stage, systems should be restored back to the pre-incident condition, although necessary action should then be performed to address any vulnerabilities exploited as part of the original data breach. This may involve activities such as installing software patches, changing all staff passwords, changing firewall settings and amending procedures.

Notification

The notification of a **Data Breach** and resulting loss of data is a sensitive issue that must be handled carefully and with full management approval. The **Data Breach Team** leader will decide, based on legal and other expert advice and from as full an understanding of the impact of incident as possible, what statutory notification is required and the form that statutory notification will take.

It is important that you always comply in full with applicable legal and regulatory requirements regarding **Data Breach** notification and carefully assess whether any offerings could be to be made to **Data Subjects** that may be impacted by the incident, such as credit monitoring services.

Records collected as part of the **Data Breach** response may be required as part of any resulting investigations by the relevant regulatory bodies.

The **Data Breach** formal notification process can begin by telephoning the **Information Commissioner's Office** (**ICO**) on 0303 123 1113.

Post Incident Activity

The **Data Breach Team** leader will decide, based on the latest information from the Incident Liaison and other members of their team, the point at which response activities should be ceased and the **Data Breach Response Team** stood down. Note that the recovery and execution of plans may continue beyond this point, but under less formal management control.

This decision will be up to the **Data Breach Team** leader's judgement but should be based upon the following criteria:

- the situation has been fully resolved or is reasonably stable
- the pace of change of the situation are slowed to a point where few decisions are required
- the appropriate response is well underway and recovery plans are progressing and to schedule
- the degree of risk to the business has lessened to an acceptable point
- immediate legal and regulatory responsibilities have been fulfilled

If recovery from the incident is ongoing, the **Data Breach Team** leader should define the next actions to be taken. These may include:

- less frequent meetings of the **Data Breach Response Team**, e.g. weekly or monthly, depending on the circumstances
- informing all involved parties that the **Data Breach Response Team** is standing down
- ensuring all documentation of the incident is complete and has been secured
- requesting all staff not involved in further work should return to normal duties

All actions taken as part of standing down should be recorded.

After the **Data Breach Response Team** has been stood down, the **Data Breach Team** leader will de-brief all members, ideally within 24 hours. Relevant records of the incident will be examined by the **Data Breach Response Team** to ensure that they reflect actual events and represent a complete and accurate record of the data breach and responses taken.

Any immediate concerns or feedback from the team will be recorded.

A more formal post **Data Breach** review may be held at a time to be decided by senior management of your organisation, according to the magnitude and nature of the **Data Breach**.

Do I need an EU or UK GDPR agent?

The short answer is it depends...

If your organisation is based in the UK, you don't actively seek clients within the EU, your only permanent place of business is within the UK, and you don't have any employees within the EU, then you only need to worry about UK GDPR and have no need for either a UK or EU agent.

Similarly, if your organisation is based in the EU, you don't actively seek clients within the UK, your only permanent place of business is within the EU, and you don't have any employees within the UK, then you only need to worry about GDPR and have no need for either a UK or EU agent.

However, if your organisation is based in the UK, and you do actively seek clients within the EU and/or you have employees within the EU, then you do need an EU agent.

If your organisation is based in the EU, and you do actively seek clients within the UK and/or you have employees within the UK, then you need a UK agent.

If your organisation is based outside of the UK and the EU, you actively seek clients within the UK and EU, and your only place of business is outside of the UK and EU, then you need both a UK agent and an EU agent.

So, what does an EU and/or UK agent actually do?

The role of the EU and/or UK agent is to act as the interface between you, and the relevant **Data Protection Authority (DPA)**, who is the Information Commissioner (**ICO**) in the UK. Outside of the UK you will need to check who the relevant **Data Protection Authority** is for the country where your EU agent is based.

So, are they responsible for me implementing GDPR correctly and remaining compliant?

No. It is not the EU and/or UK agent's role to provide you with GDPR training or consultancy, the responsibility for ensuring your organisation is compliant with GDPR / UK GDPR remains with you.

Legal precedent has established this to be the case. If the Data Protection Authority within the country where your EU / UK agent is registered finds a fault in your GDPR implementation and imposes a penalty or they impose a penalty following a data breach, responsibility for paying that penalty remains with you, the EU / UK agent bears no responsibility

So, if they are not liable, why do I need one?

The short answer is to protect you from concurrent penalties (so you should think of them as an insurance policy).

Let's take an example, you are a UK company, and you have clients right across Europe, in all 27 EU countries, but you don't have an EU agent.

You have a data breach, and the UK ICO imposes a penalty on you for £1000 in respect of this breach. Each EU country where you have clients can now also impose a penalty for this same breach, so suddenly your penalty isn't £1000 it's now gone up by a further £27,000.

Let's take the same scenario, but now you have an EU agent (for the sake of this example, your EU agent is registered in the Netherlands).

Now, you have the same data breach. The UK ICO imposes a penalty of £1000. The Dutch data protection authority

(**DPA**) also imposes a penalty of £1000. You cannot receive a penalty from any other EU country as you have established your EU point of presence in the Netherlands by appointing your agent there. So instead of £28,000, your penalty is now just £2,000. Suddenly, the fee your EU agent charges you seems like a really good investment.

So how much should an EU or UK agent cost my organisation?

For EU agents, you shouldn't expect to pay more than € 1,500 - € 2,000 per annum

For UK agents, again you shouldn't expect to pay more than £1,000 to £2,000 per annum.

For more details of where to find a UK or EU agent, please see the Useful Resources section of this book.

Fees and Penalties

While all organisations who handle personal data within the UK have to register with the Information Commissioner's Office (ICO), not everyone has to pay an annual registration fee.

The ICO has a useful self-assessment form at https://ico.org.uk/for-organisations/data-protection-fee/

If you do need to pay a fee, two factors are important in determining your fee, your annual turnover, and the number of employees within your organization.

If you have 10 or fewer employees OR your turnover is less than £632,000 then the fee is £40 per annum (£35 if paid by Direct Debit).

If you have 10 or more employees but fewer than 250 employees OR your turnover is less than £26m then the fee is £60 per annum (£55 if paid by Direct Debit)

If you have 250 employees or more OR your turnover is in excess of £26m then you have to pay £2900 per annum (£2895 if paid by Direct Debit).

It is really important that you register with the ICO. If you should be registered but fail to do so, or you fail to renew your annual licence fee, you can be fined between £400 and £4,000 in addition to any licence fee which may be due.

For any other breaches of UK GDPR, you can be fined up to 4% of your global turnover or £18m whichever is the higher.

So, what of the future?

The UK Department for Digital, Culture, Media & Sport ('DCMS') announced, on 9 September 2021, that the Government had launched a public consultation, proposing reform to the UK's data protection regime, aiming to deliver Mission 2 of the National Data Strategy to secure a pro-growth and trusted data regime. In particular, the reform proposals include reforming the accountability framework and related requirements established under the **General Data Protection Regulation** (Regulation (EU) 2016/679) ('**GDPR**') and changes to cookie and data transfer rules.

Accountability reforms

Further to the above, the reform proposals specifically include:

reforming the accountability framework by implementing a more flexible and risk-based framework which is based on privacy management programs.

Under this framework, organisations would be required to implement a privacy management program tailored to their processing activities and ensure data privacy management is embraced holistically rather than just as a 'box-ticking' exercise. To achieve this, the consultation notes that some specific compliance requirements in the **UK General Data Protection Regulation** ('**UK GDPR**') would be amended or removed.

These proposals include:

removing the existing requirements to designate a **Data Protection Officer** ('**DPO**') and authorising individual organisations to determine such requirements based on their discretion;

removing the requirement for organisations to undertake a **Data Protection Impact Assessment** ('**DPIA**'), so that organisations may adopt different approaches to identify and minimise data protection risks that better reflect their specific circumstances.

In addition to this, the consultation proposes removing the requirement for prior consultation with the **Information Commissioner's Office** ('**ICO**') upon identification of a high risk data processing, but rather encourage a more proactive, open, and collaborative dialogue between organisations and the **ICO**;

removing record keeping requirements under Article 30 of the **UK GDPR**, while granting organisations more flexibility about how to keep certain records in a way that reflects the volume and sensitivity of the **Personally Identifiable Information** they handle, and the type(s) of data processing they carry out;

changing the threshold for reporting a **Data Breach** to the **ICO** so that organisations must report a **Data Breach**, unless the risk to individuals is not material.

Cookies and electronic communications

The proposed reforms related to cookies and electronic communications include the following:

permitting organisations to use analytics cookies and similar technologies without the user's consent, thereby treating such cookies in the same way as 'strictly necessary' for which consent is not required.

The consultation also outlines a second option for tackling the identified issues and welcomes evidence on the risks and benefits of a second option; i.e. permitting organisations to store information on, or collect information from, a user's device without their consent for other limited purposes; and extending the soft opt-in to electronic communications from organisations other than businesses where they have previously formed a relationship with the person, perhaps as a result of membership or subscription.

Additional proposed reforms

Other notable reforms proposed by the Government include:

creating a new condition within Schedule 1 to the **Data Protection Act 2018** which specifically addresses the processing of sensitive personal data as necessary for bias monitoring, detection, and correction in relation to **AI** systems;

consolidating and bringing together research-specific provisions and incorporating a clearer definition of scientific research, among others.

This proposal follows stakeholders' concerns regarding the fact that **UK GDPR** can create barriers to responsible innovation because of the ambiguity of some definitions and lack of explanatory case law or regulatory guidance, particularly with regards to the rules for using and re-using data for research purposes;

creating a limited, exhaustive list of **Legitimate Interests** for which organisations can use **Personally Identifiable Information** without applying the balancing test in order to give them more confidence to process personal data without unnecessary recourse to consent.

Data transfers

The consultation reiterates the Government's intention to reform the **UK**'s data transfer regime.

Notably, the consultation outlines the Government's intention to add more countries to the list by progressing an ambitious program of adequacy assessments in line with the **UK**'s global ambitions and commitment to high standards of data protection.

Furthermore, the consultation notes the Government's intention to relax the requirement to review adequacy regulations every four years, as well as explore amendments to the international transfers regime to give organisations greater flexibility in their use of transfer mechanisms.

ICO reforms

The consultation proposes a new governance model for the **ICO**, including introducing a new, statutory framework that sets out the strategic objectives and duties that the **ICO** must fulfil when exercising its functions, introducing a power for the Secretary of State for DCMS to prepare a statement of strategic priorities to inform how the **ICO** sets its own regulatory priorities, and establishing an independent board and a CEO at the **ICO**.

In response to the consultation, on 9 September 2021 the **ICO** published a statement from the **Information Commissioner**, Elizabeth Denham, who welcomed the Government's intention to ensure a legislative framework that is fit for the future, and noted that the **ICO** will provide constructive input and feedback as the work progresses, including through their public response to the consultation, ensuring that the **ICO** can effectively regulate this legislation.

The consultation closes on 19 November 2021.

I was fortunate to have a discussion with Rt Hon Damian Hinds MP, the UK Security Minister regarding the proposed changes. Understandably, he emphasised that this was only a consultation and not a White Paper. As such, there is no guarantee that any of the suggestions in the consultation will ever be enacted in legislation.

So my personal feel is that given that the consultation closes in November 2021, given the volume of anticipated responses, it will be April/May 2022 before all of the responses have been analysed.

If from that we assume that a White Paper emerges in the Autumn of 2022, by the time it has made its way through an already congested Parliamentary programme, it is unlikely to become legislation and receive royal assent until mid 2023. Whether that happens of course, depends on whether the Prime Minister decides to allow this Parliament to run its full course to 2024, or whether they will seek to call an early General Election in 2023.

So, I will be keeping a close watching brief on the outcome of the consultation and subsequent steps (if any). You can keep up to date on the latest developments by subscribing to my GDPR Weekly Show podcasts, or join me on Clubhouse every Thursday at 4pm UK time for the GDPR Weekly Show live forum.

Clearly, if there are major modifications to UK GDPR, I will produce a new edition of this book!

Useful resources

Templates

You can find all the templates mentioned throughout this book available for download at https://www.gdprmadesimple.club/templates

UK Agents

We are always happy to act as the UK agent for your organisation, whether you are based inside or outside of the EU. For more details please see https://www.gdprmadesimple.club/uk-agents

EU Agents

We can put you in touch with several organisations who provide EU agent services. For more details please see https://www.gdprmadesimple.club/eu-agents

Useful information

Another useful source of information is the Information Commissioner's website which you can find at https://www.ico.org.uk

Useful equipment

You can find suitable GDPR / UK GDPR compliant cross-cut shredders at https://www.gdprmadesimple.club/shredders

Sample Privacy Policy

Suitable wording for a UK GDPR compliant Privacy Policy is given below. This wording is also available via our Templates library which you can access at https://www.gdprmadesimple.club/templates

Please note that this wording was correct at the time of initial publication (October 2021) but may have subsequently been updated, so we would always advise checking our Template library for the latest wording.

Privacy Policy

This is the privacy notice of [enter your organisation name here]. In this document, "we", "our", or "us" refers to [enter your organisation name here].

Introduction

This privacy notice aims to inform you about how we collect and process any information that we collect from you, or that you provide to us. It covers information that could identify you ("personal information") and information that could not. In the context of the law and this notice, "process" means collect, store, transfer, use or otherwise act on information. It tells you about your privacy rights and how the law protects you.

We are committed to protecting your privacy and the confidentiality of your personal information. Our policy is not just an exercise in complying with the law, but a continuation of our respect for you and your personal information.

We undertake to preserve the confidentiality of all information you provide to us.

Our policy complies with the Data Protection Act 2018 (Act) accordingly incorporating the EU General Data Protection Regulation (GDPR) and UK General Data Protection Regulation (UK GDPR). UK GDPR applies to any data we collect after 11 pm on 31st December 2020.

The law requires us to tell you about your rights and our obligations to you regarding the processing and control of your personal data.

Except as set out below, we do not share, or sell, or disclose to a third party, any information collected through our website.

1. Data we process

We may collect, use, store and transfer different kinds of personal data about you. We have collated these into groups as follows:

Your identity information includes items such as first name, last name, title, date of birth, and other identifiers that you may have provided at some time.

Your contact information includes information such as billing address, delivery address, email address, telephone numbers and any other information you have given to us for the purpose of communication or meeting.

Your financial data includes information such as your bank account and payment card details.

Transaction data includes details about payments or communications to and from you and information about products and services you have purchased from us.

Technical data includes your internet protocol (IP) address, browser type and version, time zone setting and location, browser plug-in types and versions, operating system and platform and other technology on the devices you use to access this website.

Marketing data includes your preferences in receiving marketing from us; communication preferences; responses and actions in relation to your use of our services.

We may aggregate anonymous data such as statistical or demographic data for any purpose.

Anonymous data is data that does not identify you as an individual. Aggregated data may be derived from your personal data but is not considered personal information in law because it does not reveal your identity.

For example, we may aggregate profile data to assess interest in a product or service.

However, if we combine or connect aggregated data with your personal information so that it can identify you in any way, we treat the combined data as personal information, and it will be used in accordance with this Privacy Policy.

2. Special personal information

Special personal information is data about your race or ethnicity, religious or philosophical beliefs, sex life, sexual orientation, political opinions, trade union membership, information about your health and genetic and biometric data.

It also includes information about criminal convictions and offences.

We may only collect special personal information about you if there is a lawful basis on which to do so. If we do this, we will inform you of the lawful bases which apply.

3. If you do not provide personal information we need

Where we need to collect personal data by law, or under the terms of a contract we have with you, and you fail to provide that data when requested, we may not be able to perform that contract. In that case, we may have to stop providing a service to you. If this occurs, we will notify you of this at the time.

The bases on which we process information about you

The law requires us to determine under which of six defined bases we process different categories of your personal information, and to notify you of the basis for each category.

If a basis on which we process your personal information is no longer relevant, then we shall immediately stop processing your data.

If the basis changes, then if required by law we shall notify you of the change and of any new basis under which we have determined that we can continue to process your information.

4. Information we process because we have a contractual obligation with you

When you create an account on our website, buy a product or service from us, or otherwise agree to our terms and conditions, a contract is formed between you and us.

In order to carry out our obligations under that contract we must process the information you give us. Some of this information may be personal information.

We may use it in order to:
- verify your identity for security purposes
- sell products to you
- provide you with our services
- provide you with suggestions and advice on products, services and how to obtain the most from using our website

We process this information on the basis there is a contract between us, or that you have requested we use the information before we enter into a legal contract.

We shall continue to process this information until the contract between us ends or is terminated by either party under the terms of the contract.

5. Information we process with your consent

Through certain actions when otherwise there is no contractual relationship between us, such as when you browse our website or ask us to provide you more information about our business, including our products and services, you provide your consent to us to process information that may be personal information.

Wherever possible, we aim to obtain your explicit consent to process this information, for example, by asking you to agree to our use of cookies.

If you have given us explicit permission to do so, we may from time to time pass your name and contact information to selected associates whom we consider may provide services or products you would find useful.

We continue to process your information on this basis until you withdraw your consent, or it can be reasonably assumed that your consent no longer exists.

You may withdraw your consent at any time by instructing us at [enter your contact email here]. However, if you do so, you may not be able to use our website or our services further.

6. Information we process for the purposes of legitimate interests

We may process information on the basis there is a legitimate interest, either to you or to us, of doing so.

Where we process your information on this basis, we do so after having given careful consideration to:
- whether the same objective could be achieved through other means
- whether processing (or not processing) might cause you harm
- whether you would expect us to process your data, and whether you would, in the round, consider it reasonable for us to do so.

For example, we may process your data on this basis for the purposes of:
- record-keeping for the proper and necessary administration of our business
- responding to unsolicited communication from you to which we believe you would expect a response
- protecting and asserting the legal rights of any party
- insuring against or obtaining professional advice that is required to manage business risk
- protecting your interests where we believe we have a duty to do so

7. Information we process because we have a legal obligation

Sometimes, we must process your information in order to comply with a statutory obligation.

For example, we may be required to give information to legal authorities if they so request or if they have the proper authorisation such as a search warrant or court order.
This may include your personal information.

Specific uses of information you provide to us

8. Information provided on the understanding that it will be shared with a third party

Our website allows you to post information with a view to that information being read, copied, downloaded, or used by other people.

Examples include:
- [posting a message to our forum]
- [tagging an image]
- [clicking on an icon next to another visitor's message to convey your agreement, disagreement, or thanks]

In posting personal information, it is up to you to satisfy yourself about the privacy level of every person who might use it.

We do not specifically use this information except to allow it to be displayed or shared.

We do store it in line with our Data Retention policy. A copy of our Data Retention policy is available on demand – please contact [enter your contact email here]

Once your information enters the public domain, we have no control over what any individual third party may do with it. We accept no responsibility for their actions at any time.

Provided your request is reasonable and there is no legal basis for us to retain it, then at our discretion we may agree to your request to delete personal information that you have posted. You can make a request by contacting us at [enter your contact email here]

9. Information relating to your method of payment

We take the following measures to protect your payment information:
- Payments are processed via a third-party processor [Name of payment processor here]. We do not keep payment information on our servers so as:
1. to prevent the possibility of our duplicating a transaction without a new instruction from you.
2. to prevent any other third party from carrying out a transaction without your consent

10. Communicating with us

When you contact us, whether by telephone, through our website or by e-mail, we collect the data you have given to us in order to reply with the information you need.
We record your request and our reply in order to increase the efficiency of our business.
We keep personally identifiable information associated with your message, such as your name and email address so as to be able to track our communications with you to provide a high-quality service.

11. Complaining

When we receive a complaint, we record all the information you have given to us.

We use that information to resolve your complaint.

If your complaint reasonably requires us to contact some other person, we may decide to give to that other person some of the information contained in your complaint. We do this as infrequently as possible, but it is a matter for our sole discretion as to whether we do give information, and if we do, what that information is.

We may also compile statistics showing information obtained from this source to assess the level of service we provide, but not in a way that could identify you or any other person.

12. Affiliate and business partner information

This is information given to us by you in your capacity as an affiliate of us or as a business partner.

It allows us to recognise visitors that you have referred to us, and to credit to you commission due for such referrals. It also includes information that allows us to transfer commission to you.

The information is not used for any other purpose.

We undertake to preserve the confidentiality of the information and of the terms of our relationship.

We expect any affiliate or partner to agree to reciprocate this policy.

Use of information we collect through automated systems when you visit our website

13. Cookies

Cookies are small text files that are placed on your computer's hard drive by your web browser when you visit any website. They allow information gathered on one web page to be stored until it is needed for use on another, allowing a website to provide you with a personalised experience and the website owner with statistics about how you use the website so that it can be improved.

Some cookies may last for a defined period of time, such as one day or until you close your browser. Others last indefinitely.

Your web browser should allow you to delete any you choose. It also should allow you to prevent or limit their use.
Our website uses cookies. They are placed by software that operates on our servers, and by software operated by third parties whose services we use.

We use cookies in the following ways:
- to track how you use our website
- to record whether you have seen specific messages we display on our website
- to keep you signed in our site
- to record your answers to surveys and questionnaires on our site while you complete them

14. Personal identifiers from your browsing activity

Requests by your web browser to our servers for web pages and other content on our website are recorded.

We record information such as your geographical location (limited to town/city), your Internet service provider and your IP address. We also record information about the software you are using to browse our website, such as the type of computer or device and the screen resolution.

We use this information in aggregate to assess the popularity of the webpages on our website and how we perform in providing content to you.

If combined with other information we know about you from previous visits, in exceptional circumstances, this data possibly could be used to identify you personally. Where this occurs, your data will be treated in confidence as per the information in this Privacy Policy.

15. Our use of re-marketing

Re-marketing involves placing a cookie on your computer when you browse our website in order to be able to serve to you an advert for our products or services when you visit some other website.

We may use a third party to provide us with re-marketing services from time to time. If so, then you may see advertisements for our products and services on other websites.

Disclosure and sharing of your information

16. Information we obtain from third parties

Although we do not disclose your personal information to any third party (except as set out in this notice), we sometimes receive data that is indirectly made up from your personal information from third parties whose services we use.

17. Third party advertising on our website

Third parties may advertise on our website. In doing so, those parties, their agents or other companies working for them may use technology that automatically collects information about you when their advertisement is displayed on our website.

They may also use other technology such as cookies or JavaScript to personalise the content of, and to measure the performance of their adverts.

We do not have control over these technologies or the data that these parties obtain.

Accordingly, this privacy notice does not cover the information practices of these third parties.

18. Credit reference

To assist in combating fraud, we share information with credit reference agencies, so far as it relates to clients or customers who instruct their credit card issuer to cancel payment to us without having first provided an acceptable reason to us and given us the opportunity to refund their money.

Control over your own information.

19. Your duty to inform us of changes

It is important that the personal data we hold about you is accurate and current. Please keep us informed if your personal data changes.

20. Access to your personal information

At any time, you may review or update personally identifiable information that we hold about you, by signing into your account on our website.

To obtain a copy of any information that is not provided on our website you should contact us via [enter your contact email here]to make that request.

After receiving the request, we will tell you when we expect to provide you with the information, and whether we require any additional information from you to prove your identity.

There is normally no charge for providing this information. However, we may make a charge of up to £100 if the request for information is vexatious or we have previously provided the requested information to you.

21. Removal of your information

If you wish us to remove personally identifiable information from our website, you should contact us to make your request.

This may limit the service we can provide to you.

22. Verification of your information

When we receive any request to access, edit or delete personal identifiable information we shall first take reasonable steps to verify your identity before granting you access or otherwise taking any action. This is important to safeguard your information.

Other matters

23. Use of site by children

We do not sell products or provide services for purchase by children, nor do we market to children.

If you are under 13, you may use our website only with consent from a parent or guardian.

26. How you can complain

If you are not happy with our Privacy Policy or if you have any complaint, then you should tell us via email to [enter your contact email here]

If a dispute is not settled, then we hope you will agree to attempt to resolve it by engaging in good faith with us in a process of mediation or arbitration.

If you are in any way dissatisfied about how we process your personal information, you have a right to lodge a complaint with the Information Commissioner's Office (ICO). This can be done by writing to them at Information Commissioner's Office, Wycliffe House, Water Lane, Wilmslow, Cheshire, SK9 5AF or telephone 0303 123 1113. We would, however, appreciate the opportunity to talk to you about your concern before you approach the ICO.

27. Retention period for personal data

Except as otherwise mentioned in this privacy notice, we keep your personal information only for as long as required by us:
- to provide you with the services you have requested.
- to comply with other law, including for the period demanded by our tax authorities.
- to support a claim or defence in court

Further details of our data retention are detailed in our Data Retention policy. You can obtain a copy of our Data Retention policy by sending an email to [enter your contact email here]

28. Compliance with the law

Our privacy policy has been compiled to comply with the law of every country or legal jurisdiction in which we aim to do business. If you think it fails to satisfy the law of your jurisdiction, we should like to hear from you via email to [enter your contact email here]
However, ultimately it is your choice as to whether you wish to use our website.

29. Review of this privacy policy

We may update this privacy notice from time to time as necessary. The terms that apply to you are those posted here on our website on the day you use our website. We advise you to print a copy for your records.

If you have any question regarding our privacy policy, please contact us via email to [enter your contact email here]

30. Date policy effective from
This policy is effective from 1st September 2021.

Glossary

We know that at times, GDPR can seem like a mass of acronyms, so hopefully this glossary will be useful in explaining what they mean: -

2FA – two factor authentication. Used in conjunction with a username and password to access a computer system. 2FA requires entry of a second piece of information usually either a security token or a biometric factor, such as a fingerprint or facial scan.

AADC – Age-Appropriate Design Code (also referred to within the UK as "The Children's Code")

AI – Artificial Intelligence

CCTV – Closed circuit television

Data Breach – an unauthorised person (either internal or external) gaining access to data within your organisation

Data Breach Register – A chronological record of every data breach (however minor) which has occurred in your organisation. See the Templates folder referenced in this book for a sample Data Breach Register.

Data Breach Response Team – the team of people within your organisation (plus any external resources) who will respond to a Data Breach.

Data Controller – means the natural or legal person, public authority, agency or other body which, alone or jointly with others, determines the purposes and means of the processing of personal data

Data Processing Agreement – the agreement between the Data Controller (or Joint Data Controllers) and the Data Processor on what Personally Identifiable Information will be transferred between the parties, how that information will be transferred and what the Data Controller is authorising the Data Processor to do with that Personally Identifiable Information.

Data Processor - means a natural or legal person, public authority, agency or other body which processes personal data on behalf of the controller.

Data Subject – a living person currently within the UK or EEA or who is normally resident within the UK or EEA

DDOS – Distributed Denial of Service, an attempt to stop a web-service from operating by sending traffic from multiple sources simultaneously

DPIA – Data Privacy Impact Assessment (often also referred to as Data Protection Impact Assessment)

DPO – Data Protection Officer. The person responsible for implementing GDPR / UK GDPR within your organisation. You may have a DPO who is internal to your organisation, external to your organisation or both.

DSAR – Data Subject Access Request

EEA – European Economic Area, which includes the following countries: - Austria, Belgium, Bulgaria, Croatia, Republic of Cyprus, Czech Republic, Denmark, Estonia, Finland, France, Germany, Greece, Hungary, Iceland, Ireland, Italy, Latvia, Liechtenstein, Lithuania, Luxembourg, Malta, Netherlands, Norway, Poland, Portugal, Romania, Slovakia, Slovenia, Spain, and Sweden.

EU - European Union, which includes the following countries: - Austria, Belgium, Bulgaria, Croatia, Republic of Cyprus, Czech Republic, Denmark, Estonia, Finland, France, Germany, Greece, Hungary, Ireland, Italy, Latvia, Liechtenstein, Luxembourg, Malta, Netherlands, Poland,

Portugal, Romania, Slovakia, Slovenia, Spain, and Sweden.

GDPR – General Data Protection Regulation

ICO – Information Commissioner's Office – see their website at https://www.ico.org.uk

Joint Data Controller - Where two or more controllers jointly determine the purposes and means of processing, they shall be joint controllers.

MFA – two factor authentication. Used in conjunction with a username and password to access a computer system. MFA requires entry of a second piece of information usually either a security token or a biometric factor, such as a fingerprint or facial scan.

PDF – Adobe Portable Document Format.

PII – personally identifiable information. Any information which can be linked to a Data Subject.

Special Category Data – this is data which GDPR / UK GDPR considers to be especially sensitive. More details of Special Category Data can be found beginning on page 26 of this book.

Standard Contractual Clauses – wording approved by the European Union to govern data transfers. You can download this wording via the URL in the **Useful Resources** section of this book.

UK – United Kingdom

URL – the address of a web page

VOIP – Voice over IP – verbal telecommunications via the Internet.

About the author

Keith Budden is an acknowledged expert in both EU and UK GDPR.

Keith has brought his expertise to over 150 organisations in the UK, Europe, South Africa and the USA.

Keith presents and produces the GDPR Weekly Show, the number 1 GDPR podcast worldwide. The GDPR Weekly Show has a new episode every Sunday morning at 9 am UK time and is available on Apple iTunes, Spotify, Amazon Podcasts, TuneIn Radio, Google Podcasts, and all major podcast platforms.

If you have an Alexa device, you can listen to the GDPR Weekly Show just by saying "Alexa, play the GDPR Weekly Show"

Keith is a regular speaker at public events and has recently spoken at The Business Networking Show in Birmingham, the International Cyber Expo at London Olympia and at a conference for the Institution of Structural Engineers.

You can contact Keith by email at keith@ensurety.co.uk or you can go to https://gdprbook.10to8.com and book a suitable time directly into his diary.